The Silent Emperor

German Emperor Frederick III

Christina Croft

© Christina Croft 2020

All rights reserved

Contents

Prologue 5
Chapter 1 – An Ornament To The Throne 7
Chapter 2 – A Negligible Quantity 17
Chapter 3 – His Love For England 26
Chapter 5 – Two Young Innocent Things 45
Chapter 6 – All That Can Be Desired 53
Chapter 7 – From God's Hand and From None Other 61
Chapter 8 – In a State of Passive Neutrality 70
Chapter 9 – Successful Villainy 80
Chapter 10 – Humble & Modest About All That He Has Done 89
Chapter 11 – Sunset From the Mount of Olives 97
Chapter 12 – No Parents Could Have Shown More Interest in Their Children 104
Chapter 13 – 'Our Fritz' 112
Chapter 14 – The Siege of Paris 127
Chapter 15 - The Crown Prince is an Imperialist 137
Chapter 16 – 'I Am Accused of Taking No Interest In Public Affairs' 144
Chapter 17 – Pain, Deep and Cruel Beyond Words ... 155
Chapter 18 – Fits of Gloom & Depression 163
Chapter 19 A Mere Branch of a German Princely Family 172
Chapter 20 – A Very Gentle Knight 179
Chapter 21 – An Ideal Prince Among Princes 187
Chapter 22 – To Suffer Without Complaint 198
Chapter 23 – Sad Reflections 206

Epilogue 212

Prologue

On a bright summer's day in June 1887, a procession of mounted kings and princes moved sedately through the streets of London in celebration of Queen Victoria's Golden Jubilee. Amid such illustrious company, all eyes were drawn to the 'towering Lohengrin-like figure' of the future German Emperor Frederick III in his imperial helmet, silver breastplate and the brilliant white uniform of the Cuirassier Guards. The cheering crowds could never have believed that he had less than a year to live, or that 'our Fritz', the hero of Koniggrätz, Worth and Sedan, would soon appear as little more than a silent portrait hanging on the walls of history.

So often throughout his life, duty, modesty and loyalty obliged him to remain silent, concealing his own achievements and stifling his opinions. Tragically, when at last he was free to speak with authority, he was rendered voiceless by a painful and debilitating illness. To those who knew him well, however, he truly deserved the epithet, 'Frederick the Noble', whose heroic stoicism in the face of suffering equalled and even surpassed his courage on the battlefield.

Chapter 1 – An Ornament To The Throne

On a dull afternoon in February 1818, twenty-three-year-old Prince William of Prussia entered his father's study, silently praying for a miracle. His friends, his tutor and his favourite aunt had warned him that his suit was hopeless, but such was his passion for his beloved Elise that he could not yield without pleading with his father, King Frederick William III, one last time.

His father's gentle features softened into a sympathetic smile as he listened attentively to William's pleas. Under other circumstances, he eventually replied, Elise would have made an ideal bride but there was nothing to be done to alter her lineage, and the Radziwills were insufficiently royal to marry into Prussia's ruling House of Hohenzollern.

The King genuinely understood how it felt to fall in love with a woman who was not 'of the blood.' Indeed, following the death of his first wife at the age of only thirty-four, he himself had secretly married the daughter of a Roman Catholic count, Auguste von Harrach, who 'lived in the fourth storey of a hotel in Frankfurt…and was so poor she had to borrow a gown to be presented in.'[1] By then, though, he had done his duty by producing a brood of legitimate sons to secure the succession; and now, much as he pitied the lovelorn young man, William, as second in line to the throne, must do likewise.

Broken-hearted but submissive, William knew that there was nothing more to be said. It was his filial and patriotic responsibility to obey the King, and he must learn to overcome his grief by committing himself wholeheartedly to his military duties.

> "I am," he told a friend, "like an orphan in a joyless, empty world. I have the sympathy of many but it affords me no consolation, on the contrary, for all

are unanimous in acknowledging the magnitude of the sacrifice which duty has imposed on me."[2]

This was more than a lament for the end of a youthful infatuation. William firmly believed that a man could ever truly love only one woman in his lifetime; and, as the years went by, Elise retained her singular place in his heart[a]. Europe was filled with suitable princesses who would gladly have succumbed to his charms, but, while he distracted himself with actresses and focussed on his military career, not one of them attracted his attention.

In 1827, however, his father decided that it was time for William to marry, as, after four years of marriage, his elder brother, Crown Prince Frederick William, still remained childless. As second-in-line to the throne William must produce an heir, and it did not take long for the King to select him an appropriate bride. That spring, William was in Weimar for the wedding of his younger brother, Charles, and the Grand Duke's daughter, Marie. In the midst of the celebrations, King Frederick William's eye fell on the bride's younger sister, sixteen-year-old Augusta, who, he decided, William would marry.

Under pressure from his father, William eventually proposed, and, in the summer of 1829, the lavish wedding took place in Berlin's Charlottenburg Palace. Guests were enchanted by the dashing groom, whose powerful physique, waves of blonde hair and striking moustache matched his reputation for bravery. At the age of only seventeen, he had won his spurs in the Napoleonic Wars, and he had gone on to display such courage at the Battle of Bar-sur-Aube that he was awarded the Prussian Iron Cross, and the Cross of St. George on direct orders from the Russian Emperor.

---

[a] When it was clear that there was no hope of marrying William, Elise became engaged to an Austrian nobleman but died of pulmonary consumption before the wedding.

Dancing in the arms of so gallant a husband, Augusta had every reason to believe that her new life in Prussia would be even more thrilling than all she had known in Weimar. At her father's court, she had been raised among scholars and poets, including Johann Goethe, who became her close friend and teacher. Since childhood, she had been encouraged to participate in intellectual conversations and political debates; and knowing of the Prussian Crown Prince's enthusiasm for poetry and art, she naively believed that her heroic young husband would be equally passionate about the arts and literature.

When the dancing was over and the celebrations faded into memories, Augusta was suddenly confronted by a disappointing realisation. She saw that she and William had virtually nothing in common, and far from viewing her as his companion and equal, he saw her merely as brood mare whom he had married out of duty. Intellectually her inferior, he spoke of nothing but the army; and he paid her so little attention that he was barely aware of her interests. When she happened to mention that there should be more statues of writers in Berlin, he replied that that was fine, provided that they were smaller than those of military heroes. If she spoke of affairs of state, he swiftly reminded her that women had no part to play in politics; and, if she disagreed with him, as was often the case, he became extremely angry and ordered her to be silent.

"In spite of all his gentleness and genuine amiability," wrote one observer, "[William] was at heart a furious autocrat and did not brook contradiction even to the smallest extent."[3]

It was humiliating enough for Augusta when he blatantly indulged his penchant for actresses, but excruciating when he expected her to entertain his mistresses. When she complained to her father-in-law, the King carelessly replied that, if she had wanted a model of fidelity, she should never have married a Hohenzollern.

If her husband was a disappointment to her, so, too, was the lacklustre court. She had anticipated glamorous receptions and intelligent conversation but instead she found the parsimonious King had no interest in balls or parties and even less desire to entertain artists or intellectuals. Although he was kind, he was a 'very ordinary man', whose court, bound by stifling rules of etiquette, reflected his lack of imagination.

> "The King neither loved, nor would tolerate the superfluous;" one contemporary writer noted. "In the circle of his family and usual guests, his table was only that of any opulent merchant; even then, he partook not of all the dishes, choosing the plainest, and those thought most wholesome."[4]

Politically, too, Prussia compared unfavourably to Weimar, which boasted one of the most progressive constitutions in Europe. King Frederick William clung tenaciously to the autocracy, refusing to delegate any of his powers. Augusta's position, Queen Victoria remarked, was 'a very difficult one. She is too enlightened and liberal for the Prussian Court.'[5]

In truth, though, Augusta did little to ameliorate her difficult situation, as, rather than trying to adapt or to please her husband, she deliberately provoked him in public. In retaliation for his flaunting of his mistresses, for example, she invited members of the Radziwill family into her entourage as a constant reminder of his doomed romance with Elise. Her behaviour rapidly alienated the court and William's family, as she sulked like a child and spoke openly of her longing to return to home, always signing her letters, 'Augusta, née Princess of Saxe-Weimar.' Her sisters-in-law despised her; and the Crown Princess could not bear to be in her company. On one occasion while attending a play, she saw Augusta enter the auditorium and sent her message ordering her to leave at once as it was inappropriate for them to be seen in the same theatre.

Her histrionics and attention-seeking even created a rift between her and her sister, Marie, with whom she developed an extreme rivalry that continued to the end of their lives. They constantly tried to outshine one another with intricate wigs and flamboyant dresses, until they almost came to blows about who had the better false teeth!

"Both ladies," wrote Princess Catherine Radziwill, "were fond of light colours and youthful attire, and spent hours in conference with their milliners, who tried in vain to induce them to wear more sober gowns and less provoking hats. They would not be persuaded, and loved to appear on State occasions wrapped in pale blue or pink draperies or Nile green frocks, with long wreaths of flowers trailing over them. They had dark and light wigs, the latter appearing generally at night, and when these were surmounted with diamond tiaras, feathers and other ornaments, the effect was truly appalling."[6]

Matters between them came to a head when Marie accused Augusta of having stolen her beloved pet tortoise. Augusta, who hated the creature, denied all knowledge of its whereabouts and, when it was eventually located in her wig, she accused Marie of having put it there on purpose to annoy her. Such an angry exchange ensued that for six months the sisters refused to speak to one another.

In the summer of 1831, a cholera epidemic spread through Berlin and, as the death toll mounted, the wealthy fled the city for their country estates. The King withdrew to his Summer Palace in Potsdam, twenty-four miles from the capital; and William and Augusta followed him, settling into Frederick the Great's New Palace – 'a huge red-brick and stucco building, with a great dark cupola on it'[7] – in the Sansoucci Park.

That summer relations between the couple were unusually cordial as Augusta was pregnant, and William eagerly anticipated the birth of a son. He was not to be disappointed. On 18th October, in her private chamber, decorated with yellow silk embroidered with Chinese figures, she gave birth to a healthy boy, whom his father named Frederick William, although to his family he would always be known as Fritz.

William was so proud of his blonde-haired, blue eyed son that he quite forgot his disagreements with Augusta, and regularly invited her to ride out in a carriage with him so they could show off the baby to the public. The truce, however, was temporary as the old disagreements soon resurfaced; and, after giving birth to a daughter, Louise ('Vivi') in 1838, Augusta declared she would have no more children, signifying that henceforth this was a marriage in name only.

Born into a maelstrom of domestic discord, Fritz' earliest impressions of the world came from the obvious disharmony between his parents. Through his infant eyes, his father was a distant and somewhat frightening, if heroic, figure, who was often absent, attending to his civil and military duties. His mother, however, was a constant presence who devoted herself to his upbringing, and, from his earliest years, instilled in him her own cultural and liberal ideas. During his infancy, she appointed two like-minded governesses: the widowed Marie von Clauswitz, a gifted painter and patron of the arts; and the Swiss Madame Godet, whose son would become Fritz's first tutor.

Shortly after Fritz' tenth birthday, Augusta began attending lectures at the renowned Joachimsthal Gymnasium so that she could select his tutors from among the most gifted professors. In February 1844, she heard a young archaeologist, Dr Ernst Curtius, give a talk on the Acropolis of Athens, and was so impressed by his knowledge and manner that she turned to her companion, the philosopher and diplomat, Frederick von Humbolt, and said, 'That is the man whom I would secure as educator of my son.'

Eight months later, on Fritz's thirteenth birthday, Curtius moved into the royal household and, for the next six years, he proved himself to be every bit worthy of the trust that Augusta had placed in him. Drawn to his affability and intelligence, Fritz became so fond of him that they developed a friendship that would continue long after he had outgrown the schoolroom. Augusta, too, found Curtius' skill as a teacher so absorbing that she often attended his lessons, not only to monitor Fritz' progress but also for her own intellectual stimulation. When the tutor suggested that his royal pupil would benefit from the company of his peers, boys of his own age were invited to join him in the schoolroom and afterwards to play robust games with him in the palace gardens. With Augusta's encouragement, Curtius regularly took Fritz to the theatre and to musical recitals; or occasionally to Berlin University to take tea with the professors and students. In the summertime, pupil and teacher spent much of their time outdoors, swimming each morning in the Havel, before riding or taking long walks along the banks of the river.

In the midst of these idyllic pursuits, Fritz was constantly reminded that he could not take his royal position for granted. Like all Prussian princes, he must learn a trade so that he could support himself in the event of a revolution. He opted for typesetting and bookbinding, and soon also became very proficient at carpentry. Like all Prussian princes, too, when he was seven years old, he began extensive military training. His father's aide-de-camp, Colonel von Unruh, was named as his military governor; and, the following year, a drill sergeant was appointed to teach him and two friends, Rudolf von Kastrow and Adolf Konismark, the rudiments of army discipline. On his tenth birthday came the proud moment when his grandfather, the King, commissioned him into the 1st Regiment of the Infantry of the Guard.

> "You are but a little fellow as yet, Fritz," the King gently told him, "but do your best to get to know these gentlemen, and some day you will be their overseer, however much they may now see over you."[8]

Beyond the classroom and the military training, Fritz occasionally attended public functions, and spent time with his large extended family. He was fond of his uncle, Crown Prince Frederick William, a skilled craftsman with a particular interest in architecture. The Crown Princess, too, developed a strong bond of affection with her nephew, despite her ongoing antipathy towards his mother. Less reputable were his father's younger brothers, Charles and Albrecht, both of whom were renowned philanderers with a proclivity for making 'ill-timed, improper jokes'[9] and 'unsuitable' conversation. Fritz was repelled by Charles; and thought Albrecht disgusting when, tired of his cruelty and infidelity, his wife, Marianne of the Netherlands, left him to take up with her former coachman. The more sensitive Crown Prince despaired of his brothers' behaviour, remarking that if they had been the sons of a petty official rather than a king, 'I should have become an architect, William an N.C.O., Charles would have gone to prison, and Albrecht would have become a drunkard.'[10] Queen Victoria agreed that Charles was 'a very wicked man…very immoral and besides were there not some mysterious disappearances of people set to his account?'[11]

Notwithstanding the domestic tensions, Fritz was a cheerful boy with a natural affability and a sense of humour that endeared him to people of all stations. His tutor observed that he deliberated at length before taking any action but, once he had made up his mind or formed an opinion, nothing could persuade him to alter his decision.

This stubbornness was tempered by his unfailing courtesy and spontaneous kindness.

> "He possesses a simple, noble temperament," wrote the poet, Emanuel Giebel, "and a clear intellect, full of an innate regard for spiritual things. In many ways he reminds one of his grandfather but the sensible education which he has received, and which is founded upon the principle that he is not to grow up in royal seclusion, but as a man amongst men, makes one hope that someday he will, in a greater degree even than that worthy old gentleman, prove himself an ornament to the throne."[12]

There were, however, early signs of contradictions in his character for, while he was generous, and reticent about his own achievements, he was immensely proud of the Hohenzollern dynasty and acutely conscious of his position within it. Beneath his cheerfulness, too, he was prone to depression, which might have been inherited from his grandfather but more probably sprang from the mutual hostility of his parents. Torn between his mother's liberal beliefs and his father's militaristic outlook, he realised that the wisest course was to remain silent on any subject which might distress either parent. He had no desire to anger his powerful, autocratic father; and was equally reluctant to contradict his erratic mother, whose 'fluctuating moods...sway her to such an extent that sometimes when opinions differ it is wiser to pretend to agree so as not to irritate her still further.'[13]

> "[Augusta] wanted to prepare her son Frederick for his career as a future sovereign," wrote one contemporary observer, "and to help him to understand the duties which it entailed upon him, as well as to awaken his natural instincts of chivalry. [William] on the contrary, clung to the old traditions of the Hohenzollerns, which did not admit sentiment of any kind, and still less a deep

affection. The result of this state of things was that the relations between mother and son were very intimate at first…whilst those of [William] with his heir never went beyond the limits of an affection, very respectful on the one side, and sometimes very impatient on the other."[14]

These domestic tensions were compounded by a changing political landscape as the speed of industrialisation and the availability of literature gave rise to calls for greater democracy, the spread of socialist ideas and the constant threat of revolution.

Chapter 2 – A Negligible Quantity

In the spring of 1840, a rumour spread through Berlin, that, on New Year's Day, nine-year-old Fritz had been sitting on the King's knee when he said, 'What a pity it is, dear grandpapa, that you must die this year.' His words were said to have had a profound effect on the melancholic Frederick William III, and, whether or not Fritz actually made that prediction, the King's health began to deteriorate. In the early summer, he contracted a fever and died on 7th June at the age of sixty-nine. Fritz walked in the torchlight procession as his grandfather's coffin was carried to the vault of the Charlottenburg Palace for interment.

There was a notable dearth of eulogies for the departed Frederick William, who, despite his genuine kindness, had snoozed through the greater part of his reign, as an ineffectual father and an even less effective sovereign. In the 18th century, Frederick the Great had created a cultured and economically viable kingdom, but, within twenty years of his death, Prussia had suffered humiliation in the Napoleonic Wars, and King Frederick William III had done nothing to retain or restore the country's former glory.

Initially he had chosen to ignore the threat from Napoleon, preferring to maintain the kingdom's neutrality, but, in 1805, when the French invaded his territories, he formed an alliance with Tsar Alexander I and entered the conflict. On October 14th 1806, his armies were decimated at the twin battles of Jena and Auerstedt; and five weeks later, when Napoleon marched triumphantly into Berlin, he and his family fled to Memel.

> "Our houses were stripped and burnt," wrote one of his successors. "All our art treasures were absolutely destroyed, burnt, by Napoleon…We now must re-create, rebuild almost from the beginning."[15]

By the terms of the Treaty of Tilsit, Frederick William ceded a large part of his territory to the French, and, to meet the high cost of the occupying army, he was forced to sell many of his possession, including his wife's jewels. The Queen was so fearful and stressed that her health soon broke down, and, in June 1810, she died in her husband's arms.

Five years later, following Napoleon's ultimate defeat at Waterloo, a congress was held in Vienna to re-establish national borders in the hope of ensuring a lasting peace throughout Europe. Representatives from Russia, France, Britain and Austria set out their demands, but no one took Frederick William seriously and 'not one Prussian managed to get his voice heard.'[16] Fortunately for the King, the Tsar proved to be a faithful ally, and, thanks solely to his intervention, Prussia gained the greater part of Saxony, Posen, Danzig and the Rhineland.

Throughout the remaining twenty-five years of his reign, the well-meaning but unimaginative King did so little to improve his country's prestige that, by 1840, 'Prussia was treated by Europe as a negligible quantity.'[17] In foreign affairs, he was content to rely completely on Russia; and, domestically, he promised but failed to deliver a constitution. The kingdom's crumbling infrastructure reflected his apathy, as the dingy and dilapidated capital epitomised his jaded monarchy. Open drains and sewers ran down the rickety cobbled streets, and in the summer months the stench was overwhelming. A British diplomat complained that he was depressed by the foul-smelling air, flat landscape and drab buildings; and the Swiss journalist, Maximilian Harding, was disgusted by the 'a narrow, dirty river, narrow streets with open gutters, rarely a green spot within the municipality.'[18]

With the death of Frederick William III, the kingdom was ripe for renewal, and when Fritz' uncle ascended the throne as Frederick William IV, a spirit of optimism spread through the population. 'Fat and tall [and looking] like a good-natured farmer,'[19] he began his reign well: pardoning all political prisoners; removing press censorship; and promising a constitution to give power to an elected assembly.

From across the sea, Queen Victoria watched these events with interest, hoping that a new and more liberal Prussia would be less reliant on Russia and more inclined towards Britain. She had never trusted the Russians, and her ministers feared the Tsar could hinder British interests in India, and it would, therefore, be beneficial if she could entice Frederick William IV away from his eastern ally. To that end, in 1843, she invited the King to England to stand as godfather to her infant son, Albert Edward ('Bertie'), the Prince of Wales. Throughout his visit, Frederick William made a favourable impression on the Queen, who thought him 'so kind and well-meaning...a very delightful person, amusing, clever and amiable.' Her subjects were equally impressed when he honoured a promise that he had made to the reformer, Elizabeth Fry, by accompanying her to Newgate Prison to attend a religious service and meet some of the female prisoners.

Prince Albert made use of the visit to describe to Frederick William his vision for German unification. At the time, Germany comprised a series of independent duchies and kingdoms, and, for many years there had been discussions about the benefits of unification. The predominantly Catholic southern states favoured a 'greater Germany' – a union of all German-speaking peoples led by Austria and based loosely on the old Holy Roman Empire; while the Protestant states in the north preferred a 'lesser Germany', independent of Austria and led by Prussia. Prince Albert had written a treatise on the subject of a lesser Germany, and contended that Prussia could win the support of the southern states by replacing the autocracy with a constitutional monarchy.

Frederick William listened politely and expressed genuine interest in Prince Albert's ideas, but he had no intention of surrendering any of his autocratic powers for fear of diminishing the status of the monarchy. He 'devoutly desired improvement, reform, renovation,' his ambassador to England observed, 'but could only conceive of such, as should in every point proceed from the dictation of the Crown.'[20] His insistence on maintain the autocracy crushed the liberals' hopes of reform, and, within three years of his accession, the optimism that had characterised the start of his reign had dissolved into division and frustration.

> "Every Prussian monarch ascends the throne under the evil condition that the Prussian State in its present form is a wholly artificial one," wrote one contemporary author. "The population is as much an aggregation of shreds and patches as their abode. There is no dominating sense of unity among them, and the heir of any throne which is based on a loose rubble of popular materials, instead of on a sound nationality, is much to be pitied. Prussia in her present limits is an artificial state, constructed for the convenience of other states; and it cannot be well governed, nor its rulers prosperous, till some one of them shows genius of that high order which can create a nationality by animating all hearts by a common impulse."[21]

Rather than showing sufficient genius to 'animate all hearts by a common impulse', Frederick William's vacillations exasperated those who had anticipated constitutional reform. The British diplomat, Lord Augustus Loftus, reported that he was, 'unable to form a decided opinion, but constantly wavering and allowing his actions to be guided by the impulse of the moment. Hence it was order, counter-order, and the natural result – disorder.'[22] He had quickly forgotten his promise to create a democratic legislature, and seven years passed before financial necessity forced him to call a national assembly, whose powers were limited to raising taxes to refill the Treasury's empty coffers.

In the winter of 1847-1848, food shortages led to a rapid rise in prices, creating a simmering resentment among the working population. A spark was all that was needed to ignite revolution, and, in February 1848, news reached Prussia that the French King Louis Philippe had been ousted from his throne and had been forced to flee to England. Unrest spread across much of Europe; and, when rioting broke out on the streets of Berlin, Frederick William wrote to Queen Victoria, urging to her join an alliance to take concerted action to halt the spread of revolutionary feeling. The Queen politely refused on the grounds that it would create the impression of a coalition against the new French republican leaders. 'Let us therefore avoid, above all,' she replied, 'any step which could provoke them to attack the rest of Europe or could be made a pretext for doing so.'[23]

For the first time, seventeen-year-old Fritz realised the precariousness of the Prussian throne and he watched with alarm as his father sent troops into the streets to restore order. Armed with muskets, sabres and cannon, the soldiers provoked greater violence; and, on 18th March, a deputation from Cologne warned the King that unless he immediately introduced reforms, 'Your Majesty will cease to reign over the Rhenish provinces.'

Fearing a full-scale revolution, Frederick William hastily prepared a series of concessions and let it be known that he would address his people from his palace window. At the appointed time, loyal crowds gathered to hear his proclamation but, mistaking their cheers for cries of anger, he ordered two companies of dragoons into the streets to prevent a riot. As the soldiers calmly rode in single-file from the courtyard, a rifleman accidentally discharged two shots, and, although no one was hurt, word spread that the King had turned the army on the people. In the ensuing chaos, the crowds assembled barricades and marksmen fired at the troops from nearby windows. The soldiers retaliated so ferociously that, by the following morning, sixty people, including twenty dragoons, were dead.

The King desperately tried to explain that the carnage was due to a tragic misunderstanding, but the mob, refusing to be placated, placed the victims' coffins beneath his window and demanded that he and the Queen should come out to see them. The Queen was almost fainting in fear as she walked with the King into the courtyard, where he silently removed his hat as a mark of respect for the dead. He raised his voice to reiterate that the shots had been fired by accident, before promising an amnesty for everyone involved, and the immediate evacuation of the military from the city.

The humility in his tone dispelled much of the anger, and, when he had joined the mourners in a hymn for the dead, he and the Queen returned indoors unmolested. Within hours, he had honoured his promise and, as the soldiers marched from the town, the men on the barricades cheered them 'as if in acknowledgment of the bravery of brethren, and to prove no ill-will remaining.'[24]

Two days later, to the astonishment of his family and ministers, Frederick William rode into the city, waving wildly and blowing kisses to the crowds. All he wanted, he told them, was to unify Germany and promote freedom for his people. At the mention of unification, there were cheers and cries of, 'Long live the German Emperor!' but he quickly replied, 'Not so – that is not my intention.'

"The poor King of Prussia has entirely broken down," wrote Prince Albert's former mentor, Baron Stockmar. "He has never yielded or acted except when it was not only too late, but when it would have been better to do nothing."[25]

A few days later, the British diplomat, Sir Stratford Canning, arrived in Berlin and found it almost deserted. In the absence of the military, only a few weary burghers armed with muskets patrolled the streets or huddled into blankets to keep out the cold. After dining with the King at Potsdam, Canning concluded that:

"Never was there a more good-hearted man than he who wears the Prussian crown, with more talent and knowledge than fall to the lot of many gifted men; but alas! that which gives weight to the sceptre and dignity to the robe, and potential authority sufficient to the language of royalty, is not in proportion."[26]

The people's attitude towards Frederick William had softened, but there was no such forgiveness for Fritz' father. Prince William was held responsible for having turned the troops on the people, and was accused of trying to persuade the King to refuse to grant any concessions. The resentment against him ran so deep that the King, fearing for his safety, ordered him to leave the country and seek refuge in England. As angry mob approached his castle, he fled in disguise, and gradually managed to make his way to the home of Chevalier Bunsen, the Prussian Ambassador in London. The British received him with warmth and sympathy, which inspired in him deep fondness for the country, and affection for the British Royal Family. Baroness Bunsen later reported that, 'in no other place or country could he have passed so well the period of distress and anxiety which he had gone through, as here, having so much to interest and occupy his mind both in the country and nation.'[27]

In his father's absence, Fritz withdrew with his mother and sister to their newly-built summer palace, Schloss Babelsberg in Potsdam, where they remained undisturbed as calm gradually returned to the kingdom. While other kings had been toppled, Frederick William had retained his throne, but he was left with no vestige of authority, and he had become 'a sovereign who had virtually lost a battle against his own subjects, and who was forced to behold the people more masters of hit capital than he was himself. Not all the floods of his sentimental and vainglorious rhetoric could conceal that glaring fact.'[28]

By the time that Prince William returned to Prussia, his brother had been forced to accept a National Assembly, which led to the creation of the first Prussian Constitution and the election of a liberal government. On 1st May, the first parliament of all Germany was established in the free city of Frankfurt, and its members immediately attempted to bring about unification by offering Frederick William the title, 'Emperor of the Germans.'

The horrified Kings of Hanover, Bavaria and Württemberg raised vehement objections; and Frederick William himself was unimpressed, remarking that he could never accept a 'crown from the gutter', and only princes could make him such an offer.

His high-handed response provoked further rioting, and, when he toured the country, he was confronted by such hostility that, while visiting Saxony, he was forced to find refuge in Dresden Castle.

"Alas! Poor Germany, I am wretched about her," Queen Victoria wrote to her uncle, the King of the Belgians. "Those news from Dresden are very distressing. Really with such an excellent man as the poor King, it is too wicked to do what they have done. If only some sort of arrangement could be made; then afterwards there might be modifications."[29]

The following year, as the King entered the railway station in Potsdam, a twenty-nine-year-old former soldier, Max Joseph Sefeloge, fired a pistol at him. Fortunately, in that instant, he happened to raise his arm, deflecting the bullet that otherwise would almost certainly have killed him.

Fritz was not yet nineteen years old, but he had seen kings ousted from their thrones; riots in the streets of Berlin; his father fleeing in disguise; and the King almost fall victim to an assassin. Reflecting on these events from the haven of Babelsberg, he became convinced that Prussia needed to move towards a more democratic form of government. His mother urged him to look to Britain as a model for a future Germany, and, when his father returned home filled with praise for English hospitality, Fritz became even more enchanted by all he read and heard of the country he had yet to visit.

Chapter 3 – His Love For England

Since her accession in 1837, Queen Victoria had been eager to stay on good terms with the Prussian Royal Family; and, as Augusta's friend, she took a particular interest in Fritz' development. At Christmas and on special occasions, she sent him gifts, some of which were more welcome than others; and none so disappointed him as the kilt he received from her for his twelfth birthday. He was so angry at having been made to wear it that he promptly ripped it into shreds, declaring that he would never suffer such humiliation again.

Fortunately, the incident did not dampen his interest in Britain nor his growing fascination with the idea of a constitutional monarchy for Prussia. His father and the King, however, were determined to ensure that he understood the necessity of the autocracy, despite his mother's liberal influence and his attraction to England. During a regimental dinner in May 1849, the King's adjutant, General Leopold von Gerlach, seized the opportunity to point out to him that it was naïve to believe that Prussia could thrive as a democracy.

> "I told him how I envied him on account of his youth," von Gerlach reported, "for he would no doubt survive the end of the absurd Constitutionalism. He was of the opinion that a representation of the people would become a necessity, and I endeavoured to make it clear to him that Constitutionalism did not necessarily follow upon the absence of Absolutism."[30]

Other likeminded officials were equally quick to steer Fritz away from his mother's ideas, and none more so than a relatively young and ambitious diplomat, Otto Von Bismarck, who occasionally visited Augusta and Fritz at Schloss Babelsberg. An ardent patriot and a staunch believer in the autocracy, Bismarck was driven by the desire to make Prussia a powerful and prestigious nation.

Fritz was fascinated by Bismarck's conservation and listened to him intently but, to avoid upsetting either parent, he rarely expressed any opinion. He adopted the same approach whenever guests visited: remaining silent remained silent until he was out of his parents' earshot. One English diplomat, dining with the family, noticed that Fritz barely spoke throughout the evening but, as he was leaving, he insisted on walking him out to his carriage where he thanked him warmly for sharing such interesting opinions. Bismarck, likewise, reported that:

> "Prince Frederick…(then eighteen or nineteen years of age, but looking younger), used on these occasions to let me feel his political sympathy by warmly shaking hands with me in a friendly manner in the dusk of evening, as I was entering my carriage to take my departure, as if he were not allowed openly to express his feelings in the daylight."[31]

In 1849, at the age of seventeen, he was enrolled in the University of Bonn to read history, law and literature, and, for the first time, he felt able to speak freely with his fellow students and participated fully in all their social activities. Despite a natural reticence, he took part in several plays, once of which greatly impressed the future Queen Elizabeth of Roumania, although she thought him, 'just a little stiff in his acting, hence the staid part of the elderly man had been given him.'[32]

His favourite part of student life was the time he spent with an English barrister and author, Walter Copland Perry, who tutored him three time a week in British history, politics and literature.

> "His love for England," wrote Perry, "and his profound admiration for our Queen, were most remarkable, and tended, of course, to render our

intercourse the more interesting and confidential. Whatever information I was able to afford him about English political and social life was received by him with the greatest eagerness, and, when more solid study was concluded, we amused ourselves by writing imaginary letters to ministers and leaders of society."[33]

In 1851, he was delighted to learn that Prince Albert had invited him and his family to visit the Great Exhibition in London, but his hopes were dashed when his uncle, the King, denied them permission to leave Prussia. Frederick William IV had heard that several other princes had declined the invitation; and even members of the British establishment, including Queen Victoria's relations, had ridiculed Prince Albert's project as a dangerous waste of money. No one, they laughed, would be interested in the eclectic array of exhibits; and the great glass house – the Crystal Palace – in which they were to be housed, would probably blow down with the first gust of wind. As their laughter failed to dampen Prince Albert's enthusiasm, they began a fearmongering campaign to deter foreign visitors. So many people in one place, they said, would spread the bubonic plague and various contagious diseases; there would be rioting and food shortages; and anarchists would fill the Crystal Palace, ready to assassinate any visiting princes. Even the supportive Duke of Wellington was so alarmed that he recommended stationing soldiers around the venue; and, when the King of Hanover[b] heard that the Prussians had received an invitation, he warned King Frederick William that the British Parliament had ordered Queen Victoria and her family to stay away from London

---

[b] The King of Hanover was Queen Victoria's uncle – a son of King George III – who despised Prince Albert and resented Victoria for having inherited the British throne, which he believed should rightly have been his.

"…The Ministers as well as Prince Albert," he wrote, "are beginning to jibber with anxiety over this rubbishy Exhibition in London…I am not easily given to panicking but that I would not like anyone belonging to me exposed to the perils of these times."[34]

Horrified, King Frederick William wrote to explain to Prince Albert that, in view of the dangers, he could not permit his brother to go to England. Greatly annoyed by the King of Hanover's lies, Prince Albert curtly countered every argument, and pointed out that the rumours had been 'concocted by the enemies of our artistic and cultural venture and of all progress in civilisation, to frighten the public.'[35] Ultimately, he wrote, he could not presume to advise the King but 'any sudden postponement of the visit, and the reasons given for it, would create a very serious sensation among the public.'[36]

Unwilling to alienate a royal ally, the vacillating Frederick William finally gave way; and, on 29th April, Fritz and his family arrived at Buckingham Palace. Queen Victoria, hastening to greet them, observed that the nineteen-year-old prince was not classically handsome but he had an attractive face and beautiful blue eyes; and, in the days that followed, she was deeply impressed by his courtesy and kindly manner.

The Great Exhibition opened on 1st May, and Fritz wandered among the pink fountains and indoor trees, gazing at the magnificent Kohinoor Diamond; the newly-invented adding machines; Stephenson's hydraulic press; a tempest prognosticator[c]; and over one-hundred-thousand other exhibits from all over the world. Fascinated as he was by the splendour of the surroundings and the magical exhibits, nothing impressed him as deeply as the ease with

---

[c] A type of barometer which used leeches to predict approaching storms.

which Queen Victoria mingled with her people. When her mother became lost in the crowds, he was astounded by the Royal Family's lack of concern for her safety, or the Queen's confident assertion that she would come to no harm.

Over the next fortnight, he and his parents attended the theatre, participated in receptions, and toured the historic sights of London, where he was particularly interested in the architecture and antique treasures. Towards the end of the month, he made a two-day excursion to Wales, and paid a fleeting visit to the bustling port of Liverpool, accompanied by an aide-de-camp, Colonel Fischer, and the Prussian Consul, Burcharat. From there, he and Fischer visited Oxford incognito before returning to London to re-join the Royal Family.

All he had seen had charmed and fascinated him but nothing was more enchanting than the happy domesticity and informality in the royal household. Unlike Fritz' parents, Queen Victoria and Prince Albert were clearly devoted to one another, and they were both personally involved in their children's upbringing. While Fritz' sister, Louise, played with eight-year-old Alice and her younger siblings, the eldest child, twelve-year-old Vicky, chattered happily to her guests with a confidence beyond her years.

> "The Princess Royal…" her governess had written four years earlier, "might pass (if not seen but only overheard) for a young lady of seventeen in whichever of her three languages she chose to entertain the company."[37]

For all its attractions, London was not an ideal place to stay in summer, as all the sewage of the burgeoning population, and the malodorous effluence from factories and tanneries flowed into the stinking river. It was refreshing, therefore, to escape to the Royal Family's holiday home, Osborne House, on the Isle of Wight, where the air was sweet, the gardens green, and the private beach with its views across the Solent was the ideal spot for relaxation.

In such an idyllic setting, Fritz strolled through the gardens with Prince Albert, who described to him his hopes for a tolerant and unified Germany. For the first time, Fritz could talk freely, as he had found a kindred spirit, who not only listened but also appeared genuinely interested in his opinions. Prince Albert, too, felt a rapport with the diffident young man, for whom he quickly developed such a strong paternal affection that, before the guests left, he spoke privately with Fritz' parents about the potential benefits of a marriage between their son and his eldest daughter.

Fritz' parents responded enthusiastically but agreed that, since Vicky was still a child, it was far too soon to broach the subject with the young people. Moreover, as neither the Queen Victoria nor Prince Albert intended to force Vicky into a loveless marriage, they suggested that the best way forwards was to find opportunities of bringing the couple together in the hope that in time they might fall in love. Already, it was clear that they enjoyed each other's company, as Fritz was obviously delighted when Vicky gave him a locket containing her miniature portrait.

By the time that Fritz returned home he had fallen in love – not with the precocious little princess, but with the British way of life and the 'the domestic happiness which he found pervading the heart, and core, and focus of the greatest empire in the world.'[38] On resuming his university course, he redoubled his studies of the British constitution, and regularly exchanged letters with Prince Albert and his family.

From then onwards, while Prince Albert encouraged him to clarify his thoughts about German unification, Queen Victoria became increasingly concerned about his well-being. She had seen the problem he faced in being torn between the conflicting opinions of his parents, and wrote frankly to Augusta:

"I am always afraid in his case of the consequences of a moral clash should his father strongly recommend something and his mother warn him against it. He will wish to please both, and the fear of not succeeding will make him uncertain and hesitating and his attempts to do so will train him in falsehood – two of the greatest evils which can befall a Prince."[39]

Fritz completed his university education and rapidly progressed through the ranks and regiments of the Prussian army, all the while maintaining a regular correspondence with Vicky and her parents. Gradually, he came to the happy conclusion that one day he and Vicky would marry, but his hopes of returning soon to England were suddenly scuppered by events in the faraway Crimea.

In 1853, Tsar Nicholas I sent his troops through the Dardanelles towards Constantinople, ostensibly to protect Orthodox Christians, who were being oppressed by the Turks in the crumbling Ottoman Empire. The British, mistrusting the Russians' motives, urged the Turks to repel the invaders but, when they attempted to do so, the Russians retaliated by sinking the entire Turkish fleet in the harbour at Sinope.

Queen Victoria was appalled, and the British press condemned the 'brigand' Tsar, but King Frederick William was loth to say or do anything that could damage his relations with Russia. Convinced that Prussia alone was too weak to manage her own defences, he believed that he would need the Tsar's support in any future conflict. Fritz' father was disgusted by such a demeaning attitude and urged his brother to strengthen Prussia's military capabilities so that the kingdom could stand alone and retain full independence. Moreover, as he was eager to pursue closer ties with Britain, he had no desire to be seen to be supporting Britain's enemies or allowing Prussia to be dragged into a Russian war.

The French Emperor, Napoleon III, saw the sinking of the fleet at Sinope as an opportunity of settling a personal dispute with the Tsar[d], and ingratiating himself with Queen Victoria by proposing an Anglo-French alliance. For several months all sides struggled to reach a diplomatic solution but, by early 1854, the negotiations had reached deadlock and the British and French declared war on Russia.

Haunted by the memory of a previous Napoleon's occupation of Berlin, Frederick William was afraid to rile the French Emperor by expressing support for Russia; but, equally, he could not take up arms against his ally. Even remaining neutral was a risk, as that might make him appear weak, which could spur the French into invading the Rhineland. In a quandary, he wrote to the British Ambassador, asking Britain to guarantee the integrity of his kingdom in return for Prussian neutrality, but the British Government replied that he should join the Anglo-French alliance as the Tsar would back down in the face of such a strong opposition. At the same time, Prince Albert wrote to Fritz' father:

> "I am firmly convinced...Prussia and Germany cannot remain neutral however much Kings and Ministers may desire it."[40]

Prince William agreed, as did the Prussian Ambassador and several of King Frederick William's most trusted ministers, but, even when Austria joined the Anglo-French alliance, the King refused to listen. When the

---

[d] Louis Napoleon, a nephew of Napoleon Bonaparte, had staged a coup in December 1851 and declared himself Emperor Napoleon III of the French. The Tsar viewed him as a usurper and refused to acknowledge him as an emperor, which made him all the more desperate to flaunt Queen Victoria's recognition of his authority.

ministers persisted, he dismissed them from office, which so angered Fritz' father that he withdrew to Baden-Baden.

Queen Victoria, equally exasperated, wrote bluntly to Frederick William:

> "I have, hitherto, looked upon Prussia as one of the Great Powers which, since the peace of 1815, have been guarantors of treaties, guardians of civilisation, defenders of the right, the real arbiters of the Nations...If you, dear Sir and Brother, abdicate these obligations, you have also abdicated that position for Prussia."[41]

As usual, the King vacillated, and relations between him and Queen Victoria further deteriorated when she learned that he had permitted the transport of weapon and supplies to Russia. The British responded by sending the Royal Navy to blockade German ports for several months until Frederick William yielded and banned the sale of Prussian arms to Russia.

Frederick William's anxieties intensified in April 1855 when Napoleon III visited England and made a favourable impression on Queen Victoria. Worse was to follow four months later, when Queen Victoria visited Paris and reported triumphantly that there was now a 'complete Union of the two countries...in the most satisfactory and solid manner, for it is not only a Union of the two Governments – the two Sovereigns – it is that of the two Nations!"[42]

While Frederick William fretted and dithered, Fritz saw the prospect of marrying Vicky rapidly slipping away. The King had once told him that he would prefer him to marry a German or a Russian, and now, in view of the tensions between Britain and Prussia, he would surely not permit him to choose an English bride. Fritz longed to go at once to England to pour out his heart to Queen Victoria, but he could not leave the country without the King's permission, and to obtain that permission he would need to explain the purpose of his journey.

To his great surprise and relief, when he explained his intentions to the King, Frederick William enthused about the prospect of an English marriage. It occurred to him that, if Britain's Princess Royal were to become a Princess of Prussia, the British would prevent the French from threatening his kingdom; and he, therefore, urged Fritz to propose as soon as possible. His only proviso was that he must maintain the strictest secrecy to avoid arousing hostility from Berlin's pro-Russian faction.

Chapter 4 – A Quiet Bit of Highland Cooking

In September 1855, several Prussian journalists reported that Fritz had left Berlin for a sea-bathing holiday in Ostend, unaware that he had also made arrangements to cross the Channel incognito, with only one gentleman, Hintze, in attendance. He arrived unnoticed in Dover, and travelled by rail to Scotland, where the Royal Family was staying in the remote Balmoral Castle. By chance, Queen Victoria's cousin, the Duke of Cambridge, happened to be travelling on the same train, and the following evening, he wrote in his diary:

> "On the railroad yesterday, a young man came up and spoke to me. To my astonishment, it was the young Prince of Prussia en route to Balmoral, so evidently that marriage is to be. He came on in my carriage and pleased me very much; his views and opinions are excellent."[43]

The 'secret' visit would not remain a secret for long, and, clearly, rumours were rife about Fritz' intentions. When the Foreign Secretary, Lord Clarendon, heard what was happening, he remarked in a private letter to a friend:

> "I…hope this quiet bit of Highland cooking will succeed. It would be a good position for our young lady, who would make him a capital Queen: it would be good for Prussia and for us to be so connected, and the idea of it is such poison to the Russian party there that one feels additionally anxious for the event to come off."[44]

On Friday 14th September, Fritz arrived at Banchory not far from Aberdeen, where Prince Albert was waiting to accompany him for the final thirty miles of his journey. The Prince was in excellent spirits due to the recent fall of Sebastopol, which signified an imminent end to the Crimean War; and, on reaching Balmoral in the early evening, Fritz found the rest of the family in a celebratory mood.

As soon as she saw him, the Queen was struck by Fritz' more manly physique and his new moustache, which gave him a dashing appearance. At dinner that evening, she noticed, too, that he was more self-assured as he conversed freely with none of the shyness that had been so evident four years earlier.

For the next few days, he enjoyed all the attractions of the region: pony trekking through the rugged mountains; stalking with Prince Albert; and relishing the freedom that the remote location gave the Royal Family. In the Highlands, they walked about as freely as the lowliest crofters, calling in at the local shop for supplies; riding unguarded through the countryside; and taking a 'wee dram' of whisky with the tenants. The Liberal politician Lord Greville described 'the Queen running in and out of the house all day long, often going out alone, walking into the cottages, sitting down and chatting with the old women;'[45] and, when Fritz' aide-de-camp, Colonel Moltke arrived in Scotland in mid-September, he was astounded to discover that:

> "The most powerful monarch in the world can leave all court life so much behind. It is just plain family life here…Only one Minister is present, no doorkeepers, no army of flunkeys, not one man on guard. Nobody would guess that the Court of one of the most powerful states resides here, and that from these mountains the fate of the world is determined."[46]

In the chilly evenings, there were long conversations and card games in the tartan-walled sitting rooms, where Fritz 'afforded the Queen endless amusement by never understanding the simplest rules of vingt-et-un, explained to him on philosophic principles by Prince Albert.'[47] At dinner, he regularly found himself sitting next to Vicky, who, despite being still only fourteen-years-old, had matured considerably since his last visit. As she combined the intellectual brilliance of a highly intelligent young woman with the artless exuberance of an innocent child, it was small wonder that the American Ambassador, James Buchanan, had described her as 'the most charming girl he had ever met...All life and spirit, full of frolic and fun, with an excellent head, and a heart as big as a mountain;'[48] or that Baron Stockmar considered her 'gifted to the point of genius.'

Queen Victoria, paying close attention to Fritz' every move, was glad to hear him praise her daughter at every opportunity; and she was even more gratified to see how comfortable they were in each other's company. One eagle-eyed minister, however, who joined them for dinner observed that:

> "The little Princess Royal dined with us and looked all throughout most lovingly at him. I fancied, however, that now and then the thought flashed across her very intelligent face that he was a shade slow. I am bound to say that all the remarks I heard from him were sensible and in excellent English."[49]

Beneath all the pleasantries, Fritz was plunged into a morass of self-doubt. He longed to propose but dare not do so for fear that he would be rejected. For six days, he avoided the subject altogether until he finally summoned the courage to approach Queen Victoria and Prince Albert at breakfast. He began tentatively, telling them that he would love to be a part of their family, and, when they smiled encouragingly, he moved straight to the point and asked for permission to propose to their daughter.

Without a moment's hesitation, they gave their consent, and Fritz' relief was palpable but, as he wanted Vicky to remain as natural and unabashed as she had hitherto been throughout his visit, he asked that she should not yet be told of his intentions. Prince Albert wholeheartedly agreed; and Queen Victoria suggested that, since she would not be allowed to marry before her seventeenth birthday, they should leave her free to enjoy what was left of her childhood, and postpone the proposal until after her confirmation the following spring. The conversation concluded when the Queen firmly stated that Vicky alone would decide whether to accept or reject Fritz' proposal, as she would never be forced to marry against her will.

Although Vicky was not told of the conversation, there were several prominent figures who needed to be informed: the King of Prussia; Fritz' parents; the British Prime Minister and Foreign Secretary; and, the excited Queen could not resist telling her mother, the Duchess of Kent, and her uncle, King Leopold of the Belgians.

No sooner had the news reached Fritz' family than congratulatory telegrams began pouring into Balmoral. Several German newspapers picked up on the story, reporting that Fritz had travelled to Balmoral 'to renew his acquaintance with the eldest daughter of the Queen, who is hereafter to become his wife.'

Concerned that, if Vicky saw the reports, she would be offended to think her future was being decided, Queen Victoria abandoned the previous arrangement and urged Fritz to propose as soon as possible. To assist him, she arranged a pony trek around the remote Craig na Ban, and, when the party was some way up the hillside, the Queen and Prince Albert slowed their ponies so the young couple could ride on ahead together. Fritz dismounted and offered Vicky a sprig of white heather – a symbol of good fortune. As she took it from him, he spoke of marriage, to which she responded shyly but unhesitatingly, and, by the time they returned down the mountain, both understood that they were betrothed.

"It was not politics; it was not ambition;" Fritz later told a friend. "It was my heart."

It was Vicky's heart, too, as she saw in Fritz many of the characteristics that she most admired in her father. Both were tall and handsome with a wide-range of artistic and scientific interests; and they even shared a love of greyhounds! They both had a keen social conscience combined with a strong work ethic and an eagerness to serve their people; but, above all, Vicky had no doubt that Fritz would love her as devotedly and faithfully as her father loved her mother.

Caught up in the excitement of the moment, Queen Victoria gushed to the King of the Belgians:

"I need not tell you with what joy we accepted him… What pleases us greatly is to see that he is really delighted with Vicky."[50]

It was a sentiment echoed by Prince Albert in a letter to Baron Stockmar:

"The young people are ardently in love with one another, and the purity, innocence, and unselfishness of the young man have been on his part touching."[51]

Romance was obviously in the air that day, for, when the party returned to the castle, they learned of the betrothal of Fritz' sister, Louise, and Grand Duke Frederick of Baden. As yet, though, there would be no official announcement about Fritz' and Vicky's engagement, as it was again agreed that this would take place after Vicky's confirmation.

Fritz resumed his military duties and the months flew quickly by until he returned to England the following May for the announcement. The news was received enthusiastically across the country, and, whenever the couple appeared in public together, they were greeted with rapturous applause and cheering. Only some sections of the press reacted less graciously, as *The Times* complained that the 'petty prince' was unworthy of Queen Victoria's daughter. Other newspapers reported that the unfortunate princess was to be whisked off with unseemly haste to Berlin, where a terrible fate awaited her at the court of the Russophile, King Frederick William. In Prussia, too, there were murmurs of discontent from the pro-Russian faction, while ardent patriots, including Otto von Bismarck, feared that the marriage would anglicise the Prussian monarchy.

"You ask me…what I think of the English marriage," Bismarck wrote to a friend. "I must separate the two words to give you my opinion. The 'English' in it does not please me, the 'marriage' may be quite good, for the Princess has the reputation of a lady of brain and heart. If the Princess can leave the English-woman at home and become a Prussian, then she may be a blessing to the country. If our future Queen on the Prussian throne remains the least bit English, then I see our Court surrounded by English influence, and yet us, and the many other future sons-in-law of her gracious Majesty, receiving no notice in England save when the Opposition in Parliament runs down our Royal family and country."[52]

Fritz and Vicky were too happy and too busy to pay any attention to the grumbling, as they attended a series of public events, including a floral exhibition at the Cremone Pleasure Gardens in Chelsea. Fritz was ecstatic but, at time, Vicky appeared a little embarrassed by his attention, as one lady-in-waiting observed, 'in public he keeps looking at her, and she keeps blushing and looking the other way.'[53] Convention demanded that they should not be left alone together, and, if they went for a walk in the gardens, Vicky's parents were never more than a few steps behind them. In the evenings, they were allowed one hour 'tête-à-tête in in a room next the Queen's boudoir, with the door wide open, so that she can both see and hear what goes on.'[54]

Moreover, much of the time they were apart from one another, as Prince Albert took Fritz on a series of tours, including a visit to the Royal Arsenal in Woolwich, before heading north to Manchester, where Fritz was to make his first public speech in English. In anxious anticipation of the event, he had spent a week rehearsing, and was grateful that Vicky patiently assisted him in the correct pronunciation. His efforts were rewarded by standing ovation from his Mancunian audience.

As soon as the betrothal had been announced, Queen Victoria and Prince Albert began preparing Vicky for her future role, convinced that she would play major part in shaping a unified Germany. Each evening, Prince Albert spent an hour with her, discussing German politics and different forms of government; while Queen Victoria invited her to participate fully in official functions to familiarise her with the duties of the wife of a future sovereign.

Fritz, too, embarked on an intensive period of political training as he was given a series of placements with various ministries to learn the roles and workings of different government departments. King Frederick William also entrusted him with diplomatic missions, including representing his country at the coronation of Tsar Alexander II in Moscow[e].

On his return from Russia, he attended his sister's wedding, where, as his father struggled to conceal his sorrow at parting from his beloved daughter, his mother's expression displayed only 'conscious pride at the splendid ceremonial in honour of this match of affection.' The King, the press reported, appeared to be healthier than ever; and the Queen looked 'unusually radiant and affable…in spite of the slight defect in her gait.'

---

[e] Tsar Nicholas I died of pneumonia during the Crimean War. His successor, Alexander II, was crowned in September 1856.

Meanwhile, the British and Prussian courts were negotiating the terms of Fritz' and Vicky's marriage treaty, which involved detailed discussions about the wedding ceremony; Vicky's future household and the size of her dowry. Before the arrangements were agreed, however, King Frederick William suffered a minor stroke followed by a series of ischaemic attacks, which left him incapable of continuing the negotiations.

> "The fears of those who surrounded the King were hardly whispered;" recalled Countess Hohenthal, "but I remember that one day, when I had gone to an exhibition of modem pictures with my governess, he approached me, making some remarks about the paintings; but his tongue did not obey his will, and I was quite unable to understand what he meant."[55]

His condition left Fritz' father in an awkward dilemma as the King was obviously unfit to rule but, as his doctors hoped that he would recover, the Queen refused to consider a regency. In the meantime, the business of government could not continue in his absence, and many pressing affairs were left unresolved. The marriage negotiations were suspended until October 1857, when the King suffered an even more debilitating stroke and this time even the Queen had to admit that the situation was untenable. Reluctantly, she persuaded the King that he needed time to recuperate and should appoint his brother as his regent for a three-month period.

The wedding plans resumed and Vicky prepared her trousseau, which, among the more predictable items, contained 'twenty pairs of 'india rubber' clogs and two drawers of sponges.'[56] A dispute arose between the two courts when Prince Albert insisted that his daughter should keep control of the £40,000 dowry and £8,000 a year stipend that Parliament had awarded her. He also insisted on selecting a financial advisor for her household: his trusted friend, Ernest von Stockmar[f], whom he described as:

> "...very independent and unambitious, and so naturally depends for what he decides to do on the trust and goodwill with which he is met, and the recognition that he is serving a useful purpose; then he will do good work...I have great confidence in him, and I must credit him with being able to realise that his services are needed."[57]

The Prussians balked at the 'Coburg influence', and further disagreements arose about the ladies of Vicky's household. Prince Albert was appalled to learn that Queen Elizabeth and Princess Augusta had chosen staid older women, whom they trusted to provide them with regular reports about Vicky's behaviour, and he demanded younger companions for his seventeen-year-old daughter. Eventually a compromise was reached when Prince William recommended twenty-two-year old Countess Marie zu Lynar, and eighteen-year-old Countess Walpurga von Hohenthal.

The issue had barely been resolved when Queen Victoria was astounded to hear that the Prussians expected the wedding to take place in Berlin. Indignantly, she told her ambassador to inform the Prussian court that:

> "The assumption of its being too much for a Prince Royal of Prussia to come over to marry the Princess Royal of Great Britain in England is too absurd...Whatever may be the usual practice of Prussian Princes, it is not every day that one marries the eldest daughter of the Queen of England. The question therefore must be considered as settled and closed."[58]

No one dared to oppose her, and, despite a few grumbles in Berlin, it was agreed that the wedding would

---

[f] The son of Prince Albert's mentor, Baron Christian von Stockmar.

take place on 25th January 1858 in the Chapel Royal of St James' Palace in London.

Chapter 5 – Two Young Innocent Things

In the dark days of January 1858, Queen Victoria could hardly conceal her anguish at the thought of Vicky's departure; and it was surely more than a coincidence that Prince Albert was struck by a bout of rheumatism that left his arm almost paralysed and his hand too weak to lift a pen. Both parents strove to hide their feelings from Vicky, who was already 'dreadfully upset' at the prospect of the first 'real break in her life; the real separation from childhood' but she found some comfort in the thought of her handsome fiancé, and a letter from Fritz' sister extolling the joys of marriage:

"Since we met last," Louise had written, "my life has become so much more beautiful, more precious to me, my happiness is so much richer and deeper than before."[59]

By the middle of the month, there was no time left for nostalgia and sentimentality, as the court moved from Windsor to Buckingham Palace to welcome the numerous guests, who were arriving from across the continent. On 16th January, a large Prussian party reached London, including Fritz' parents, uncles, cousins, and members of the bride's future household. Soon, other guests arrived: the King of the Belgians; Prince Albert's brother, the Duke of Coburg; and various dignitaries and members of Queen Victoria's extended family.

Setting eyes on Vicky for the first time, her future lady-in-waiting, Walburga von Hohenthal, reported:

> "The Princess Royal, only just seventeen, was in appearance almost a child. Her radiant eyes and bewitching smile won every heart at once. She was naturally a little shy when the Queen motioned her to come forward and speak to us, but she did it with great composure and gentleness. The Prince Consort looked at her with pride and affection, for her bright intellect and quick grasp of things had

responded brilliantly to the care he had bestowed on the development of his gifted child."[60]

Far from the hustle and bustle of London, Fritz was calmly checking the suites of rooms in Berlin and Potsdam to ensure that all was in order for when he brought his bride home to Prussia. On Thursday 21st January, he set out from Berlin, and, the following evening he boarded the Royal Navy's paddle steamer, *Vivid,* for an overnight crossing to England. The next morning, a military band and a guard of honour awaited him at Dover, but, amid the music and the cheers, he did not hear the cry of two gunners, who were so badly injured by a faulty cannon while giving the gun salute, that they later had to have their arms amputated.

Twenty minutes after disembarking, Fritz was whisked away to a train bound for Bricklayers' Arms Station in London, where he was met by Prince Albert and two of Vicky's brothers: sixteen-year-old Bertie, and thirteen-year-old Alfred.

When they reached Buckingham Palace, Queen Victoria thought he looked pale, tired and nervous but he suddenly revived when he saw Vicky descending a staircase towards him. He presented her with largest row of pearls that the Queen had ever seen, but there was little time to enjoy a happy reunion with his fiancée. Lunch with numerous guests was served, followed by an equestrian display in the Royal Stables, and, after rushing back for dinner, he set out with a large royal party to Her Majesty's Theatre. Prince Albert had requested a performance of *Macbeth,* which was due to be begin at seven-thirty, but it was almost nine o'clock when Vicky and Fritz entered the theatre, prompting the audience to spring to their feet to give a rapturous ovation.

The next day, there were further gatherings with the large extended family, including a meeting with Vicky's grandmother, the Duchess of Kent, who was recovering from a mild bout of influenza. That evening came a little respite with a religious service led by Prince Albert's former chaplain, Samuel Wilberforce, the Bishop of Oxford, before Fritz withdrew to his suite in St James' Palace to spend his final night as a bachelor.

25th January dawned, bright but bitterly cold, and Fritz awoke to the news that his father had promoted him to the rank of Major General. He donned his dashing uniform and waited until resounding cheers echoed through the windows, signifying that the Queen and Vicky had left Buckingham Palace and were approaching St James'. Nervously, he waited until the Gentlemen of the Household brought word that the Queen had taken her place in the chapel, at which, flanked by his father, and his uncle, Albrecht, he walked 'with the greatest self-possession' towards the altar. Looking 'pale and much agitated', he bowed to the Queen and to his mother, before kneeling in silent prayer awaiting the bride's arrival.

At last, she appeared, trembling and leaning on her father's arm, dressed in pink silk, wreathed in flowers and crowned with orange blossom. When she had curtsied to the Queen and to Fritz' parents, he stepped towards her and, genuflecting, pressed her hand to his heart.

The words of the softly-spoken Archbishop of Canterbury were barely audible to the congregation, but 'the bridegroom's replies were heard all through the Chapel in firm and feeling accents, and dear Victoria's, though softer, were very distinct.'[61] As the service concluded with Mendelsohn's *Wedding March*, the couple and their parents were so overcome with emotion that it took several minutes to regain their composure.

"Altogether it was most gratifying and everybody seemed delighted," wrote the Duke of Cambridge, "the young couple looked well and happy and carried off their part of the ceremony remarkably well. The marriage over and the signatures affixed to the deed, we all proceeded in State to

Buckingham Palace for luncheon. The Park was crowded with people, all in the best temper and spirit, though seeing very little or nothing."[62]

Before lunch, the newly-weds appeared on the palace balcony, and, as the huge crowds roared enthusiastically, one minister took great satisfaction in recalling the press' sneering at the time of the engagement.

"The Princess Royal's wedding went off…with amazing éclat, and it is rather ludicrous to contrast the vehement articles with which the Press teemed (the *'Times'* in particular) against the alliance two years ago with the popularity of it and the enthusiasm displayed now. The whole thing seems to have been very successful."[63]

The unrepentant *Times,* however, while conceding that the wedding had gone to plan, churlishly reiterated a pessimistic warning that, if a conflict should erupt between Britain and Prussia, the poor Princess Royal would find herself in a most unenviable position.

At four o'clock in the afternoon, the couple bade farewell to their guests and set out for a two-day honeymoon in Windsor, where a group of Eton schoolboys released the horses and pulled the carriage up the hill to the castle. Finally, after all the noise, the greetings, and the frantic activity of the past few days, Fritz and Vicky were alone and unchaperoned for the first time in their lives.

Queen Victoria had adorned the bridal suite with flowers, and had arranged the letters 'V' and 'F' above the bed.

"I remember," Vicky said many years later, "how we sat here – two young innocent things – almost too shy to talk to one another."[64]

Unlike the Queen, who sent a remarkably frank description of her wedding night to her Prime Minister, Vicky left no record of her first night with Fritz, but, two days later when the court moved to Windsor, she told her mother that she was not shy with her husband and that they were perfectly happy and comfortable together.

On 28th January, Queen Victoria invested Fritz with the Order of the Garter, and, that evening, he and his fellow knights attended a grand banquet hosted by the Queen in the Waterloo Chamber. The following day, the family returned to London where the newly-weds continued to delight the crowds by their public appearances. No one who saw them had any doubt that this was a love-match, but those closest to Vicky knew the agonies she suffered at the thought of leaving her family, and, as she told the Queen, she felt it would 'kill her' to part with 'dear Papa'.

The departure day, 2nd February, inevitably arrived and, on that damp and gloomy morning, Fritz and Vicky entered the Audience Chamber of Buckingham Palace to bid her mother and siblings goodbye.

> "At 11.30," wrote the Queen's cousin, Mary of Cambridge, "we drove to the Palace to see poor dear Vicky off. It was our intention to wait downstairs; but we were sent for, and found dear Victoria surrounded by a number of crying relations in the Queen's Closet. It was a sad and trying scene!"[65]

Queen Victoria was too distressed to accompany the couple to Gravesend where they were to board the royal yacht, *Victoria & Albert,* but Prince Albert and his two eldest sons travelled with them, and, all along the route, Fritz heard the crowds calling to him, 'Treat her well or we'll have her back!'

The press reported that the couple appeared 'greatly affected' by the warmth of the crowd, but no journalists were present at the final moment of separation. Fritz and Vicky's brothers could not restrain their tears, and only Prince Albert remained stoically silent as he struggled to suppress his emotions. That evening, on returning to the palace, he wrote to Vicky:

"My heart was very full when…you laid your head on my breast to give vent to your tears. I am not of a demonstrative nature, and therefore you can hardly know how dear you have been to me, and what a void you have left behind in my heart; yet not in my heart for there you assuredly will abide henceforth as you have always done, but in my daily life, which is evermore reminding my heart of your absence."[66]

Ahead of them lay a long and tiring journey, interspersed by introductions, receptions, and celebrations at countless towns along the route. As inclement weather delayed the crossing, they reached Antwerp a day later than planned, and, on arriving in Brussels, they were expected almost immediately to appear at the King of the Belgians' ball. The dancing and dining continued until the early hours of the morning, although Fritz and Vicky had to rise at dawn to continue their journey towards Hanover. Again, the train stopped at several stations so that the couple could meet the waiting dignitaries, but they eventually reached their destination where they were met by Queen Victoria's cousin, the blind King George V. The King had arranged yet another banquet in their honour, and, much to Vicky's embarrassment, the table was set with a golden dinner service, which the King's father had taken to Hanover, despite Queen Victoria's insistence that it was the property of the British Crown. The visit was further marred for Vicky when she and Fritz visited the thirteenth-century Magdeburg Cathedral, where the crowds were 'so anxious to catch a glimpse of the Princess that her clothes, a dress of tartan velvet, were torn off her back.'[67]

The journey continued and, hour after hour, there were more stations, more formalities, more triumphal arches and more cheering crowds. There were moments of exhaustion, and moments of laughter, as when a retired Field Marshal boarded the train to offer the couple his compliments and, on being invited to sit, promptly plonked his rear into an apple meringue.

At last, on Saturday 6th February, the train reached Potsdam, where Fritz introduced Vicky to members of his extended family. Then came a brief but welcome respite as he and Vicky had a day to relax at the Babelsberg, before making their formal entry into the capital.

Monday 8th February began with a visit to the eighteenth-century Bellevue Palace to pay their respects to the invalid King, who was far more coherent than expected when, in his typically high-pitched voice, he welcomed Vicky to his Kingdom. A large military contingent had assembled to escort the couple's state coach into the city, giving the impression of a military parade rather than an extended wedding celebration. Prussian and British flags fluttered along Berlin's main thoroughfare, the *Unter den Linden,* and, as cannon boomed, the Field Marshal who had sat on the merengue, formally welcomed them on behalf of the Berlin garrison. For two hours, the procession moved slowly through the crowd-lined streets, and, as the coach windows were left open to enable well-wishers to see the bride, Vicky and her ladies shivered in their low-cut gowns in the icy February wind.

That evening, at yet another ball, the exhausted couple participated in the interminable Fackeltanz: a Polonaise performed at all Prussian royal weddings, in which the bride and groom, preceded by torch-bearing pages, gradually danced with every prince and princess in the ballroom. Fritz watched proudly as, in spite of fatigue and the strain of constantly being the centre of attention, his teenage bride performed her duties with such aplomb that, contrary to the expectations of the Russophiles, she made a very favourable impression on everyone.

"Your young Princess has occasioned an absolutely delirious enthusiasm;" wrote one observer to an English friend. "Everybody is enchanted with her sweet and joyous expression of countenance and the pleasure she shows; she has won all the hearts so ready to receive her well."[68]

For a further month, the festivities continued with endless receptions, banquets, visits and balls, until at last the fairy-tale façade dimmed, and Fritz and Vicky settled into the reality of married life in Prussia.

Chapter 6 – All That Can Be Desired

On the long, dark winter days in the gloomy Old Schloss on the Unter den Linden, Fritz gradually understood how desperately his young wife needed his guidance and reassurance. Until then, he had only ever seen her as an innocent, happy and precocious girl in the heart of a loving family, but now she had lost her familial support, and he alone must help her to adjust to an alien court in an alien kingdom. This, he soon realised, would be no easy task as she was dreadfully homesick and struggling to accept many aspects of his world that he had always taken for granted. His uncles' lewd conversations shocked her; his parents' constant bickering embarrassed her; and she disapproved of many members of his family who frittered away their time in idle gossip and frivolous distractions.

"I confess," she wrote censoriously to her father, "I could not live as the rest do here, in busy idleness, without rest, without work, doing no good…It makes me melancholy to see…existence wasted in joyless frivolity when there is so much to be done!"[69]

With her father's encouragement, she believed that she had come to Prussia to help Fritz to create a liberal, unified Germany, but it did not take her long to realise that the misogynistic court believed that women had no business interfering in affairs of state and the sole duty of a princess was to produce heirs to secure the succession. Even more disconcerting was the discovery that spies had been sent into her household to report her every movement to the Queen and Fritz' mother. When she learned that her letters were being intercepted, she was forced to find trusted bankers and diplomats, who could take them to England among their confidential or diplomatic papers.

To add to her woes, as long as the social season continued, she and Fritz would remain in living in the damp Old Schloss, with its lack of plumbing and 'huge mysterious rooms hung with dark pictures of long-forgotten royal personages.'[70] A shadowy white lady – the 'weisse frau' – reputedly haunted the gothic halls; and Vicky's rooms were separated by the 'death chamber' which, on the insistence of Fritz' uncles, had not been touched since Frederick William III died there almost twenty years earlier. Walking from her dressing room to her library meant passing by the death bed; and, as the wind howled down the chimneys and the floorboards creaked, the least superstitious person might have trembled in anticipation of a glimpse of the *weisse frau* or the old King's ghost.

Fortunately, Fritz had been granted temporary leave from his military duties, which gave him time to listen to Vicky's concerns and to offer advice when it was needed. To save her from 'busy idleness', he arranged for scientists and scholars to visit; and asked his former tutor, Curtius, to engage her in intellectual discussions. His efforts did little, though, to ease her homesickness or her habit of comparing Prussia unfavourably with England. She complained of the lackadaisical workmen; the absence of running water; the impractical design of the buildings; the frugality of the Royal Family; the paucity of silver dinnerware owned by the nobility; the fact that the Prussian children's hospitals closed at night – which was *not* the practice in England; and, with some justification, the incompetence of German dentists.

The final complaint owed much to her conversations with Fritz' father, who had, according to one visitor:

> "…been but indifferently handled by his dentist. It had become necessary to supplement Nature's handiwork by art, but so unskilfully had these, what are euphemistically termed, additions to the Emperor's mouth been contrived, that his articulation was very defective. It was almost

impossible to hear what he said, or indeed to make out in what language he was addressing you."[71]

Determined to protect Fritz from the same fate, Vicky persuaded him to take the unusual step of seeing a lady dentist.

Justified or not, however, the indiscreet comparisons did nothing to endear Vicky to the Prussians, who were unaware that, when she returned to England, she praised all things German. 'When she was in Berlin,' wrote her niece, 'everything in England was perfect: when she was in England, everything German was equally perfect.'[72]

Her brother, the Prince of Wales, agreed, remarking that, 'Vicky is always pure Prussian when she is at home, and pure English when she is in Prussia.'[73]

Even English visitors were occasionally embarrassed by her tactlessness, as a lady who met her at a ball reported:

> "The...Prince and Princess came and talked to us very kindly, but I could not help thinking the latter rather indiscreet, as when I made a futile remark as to the fine sight presented by the Palace she returned, 'A finer sight at Buckingham Palace,' then, lowering her voice, 'and prettier faces!' True enough, but a little risky addressed to a stranger with possible eavesdroppers."[74]

Many of her complaints sprang from a well-meant desire to bring about improvements, but they placed Fritz in the unenviable position of having to defend her without appearing to criticise his country. His situation was not helped by a growing tension between his wife and his mother, whose excessive demands were making life even more difficult for Vicky. Initially, Augusta was delighted to have an equally liberal-minded princess in the family, and she saw her daughter-in-law as an ally who would understand her frequent complaints about her husband and the lack of culture in Berlin. She summoned her several times a day for the most trivial of reasons, and when Vicky sighed that sometimes she was too exhausted or that it was inconvenient to drop everything to satisfy her whims, Fritz advised her to remain silent, since, 'if it keeps Mama quiet, it is in everybody's interest.'[75]

Daily, it was also becoming more apparent to Fritz how deeply Vicky idolised her father whom she saw – and described – as an 'oracle' of truth and wisdom. Much as Fritz loved and respected Prince Albert, it was difficult to accept Vicky's assertion that 'if Papa says it, it must be right'[76]; and it would be demeaning for him to appear dependent upon him. 'We are young and inexperienced in a difficult position…you will not deny your children your help,'[77] Vicky wrote to Queen Victoria, apparently forgetting that her husband, nine years her senior, was a grown man who commanded regiments and had formed his own political opinions.

Although Fritz shared Prince Albert's vision for a future Germany, he was first and foremost a *Prussian* prince who owed allegiance to the King and to his father. Moreover, unlike Prince Albert, Fritz was a soldier who enjoyed the company of his fellow officers and the time he spent with his regiment, so it was irksome when Vicky, on her father's advice, asked Prince William to relieve him of some of his military duties so that he could gain political experience in various government ministries. Unwilling to distress Vicky, Fritz remained silent, but he was undoubtedly relieved when his father indignantly ignored the suggestion.

Fritz, no less than Vicky, needed time to adjust to married life, and, to restore his equilibrium, he liked to take a walk alone every evening. This, though, soon became a matter of contention, as Vicky was loth to be parted from him even for an instant.

"I often heard her imploring him not to go;" wrote her lady-in-waiting, "but much as he gave way in everything else, he never would make that sacrifice to her."[78]

Queen Victoria was greatly alarmed when Vicky wrote plaintively that, much as she loved her husband, marriage had brought many more trials than she had expected; and Prince Albert was so concerned that he set out for Prussia to find out what was happening. Fortunately, by the time that he arrived, the couple had moved from the gloomy castle to the Babelsberg Palace in Potsdam, where Vicky's only complaint was the heat of her bedroom due to its being located above the kitchen. To Prince Albert's relief, the couple were perfectly happy together, and he was able to report to Queen Victoria that:

> "The relation between the young people is all that can be desired. I have had long talks with them singly and together, which gave me the greatest satisfaction."[79]

He was unaware at the time of the visit that his daughter was already pregnant, but, when he returned to Prussia with Queen Victoria two months later, both were delighted at the prospect of becoming grandparents. Convinced that the birth of an heir would endear Vicky to the Prussians, Queen Victoria's only regret was that she would not be able to be present during the confinement.

The pregnancy drew Fritz and Vicky closer together, and, when he resumed his military duties, they missed one another even more than either of them had expected. One of Fritz' critics scathingly remarked that he often gazed adoringly at a miniature of his wife, with tears in his eyes. For her part, Vicky, moved by the thought that she might be about to give birth to a future King of Prussia, became far more amenable to Prussian mores; and when her mother urged her to abide by English conventions for ladies in her condition, she replied that she must behave as a Prussian:

> "My first duties are here now, and in fulfilling them to the utmost I can only be doing what my own country would wish and expect."[80]

Nonetheless, as the time of her confinement approached in January 1859, Queen Victoria was so concerned about the ineptitude of Prussian obstetricians that she sent her own doctor to assist at the birth. As it happened, due to a misunderstanding, the English doctor was not informed when the princess went into labour, and Vicky was instead attended the court physician; a midwife, Fraulein Stahl; and a renowned Prussian obstetrician, Dr Martin.

Fritz was at her side throughout the harrowing and protracted ordeal, and he saw the anxious expressions on the doctors' faces when the baby was found to be in the breech position. It would have been normal practice to carry out a caesarean section, but this almost invariably resulted in the death of the mother and no one dared to risk killing a daughter of Queen Victoria. After much delay, Martin decided to use forceps and, by the time that the child was dragged from the womb, Vicky had lapsed into unconsciousness and the baby was so still and silent that the attendants feared he was dead. For over an hour, the doctor rubbed, shook and slapped the little body until at last came the sound of cry, and Fritz' anguish evaporated.

Prince William was so excited on being told of the birth of his grandson that he ran from a meeting at the Foreign Office and hailed an ordinary cab to take him to the palace; and Princess Augusta literally danced with joy, embracing everyone in her vicinity. Berlin suddenly came alive in celebration as bonfires were lit, impromptu parties were held in the streets; and Prussian and British flags were draped from windows. The excitement was equally great in England, where congratulatory telegrams poured in for the Queen and Prince Albert; and the London Opera Company added a new verse to the National Anthem in honour of Queen Victoria's first grandson.

No one, however, was quite as excited or as proud as Fritz.

"[Vicky's] charming husband delights in showing his boy ('mein Junge', he calls him) to quantities of people," wrote one Prussian lady. "…That happy young father is about everywhere, and overwhelmed with congratulations. Even the students of several Universities telegraphed that they had celebrated the joyful news by a 'salamander' (the most eccentric of all their toasts)."[81]

Further celebrations followed on the 5th March when the baby was christened Frederick *William* Victor Albert; and, responding a congratulatory message from the *Landtag*[g], Fritz cheerfully told the assembled members that, 'If God preserves the life of my son, it will be my dearest task to educate him in the feelings and principles which bind me to the Fatherland."[82]

As the winter turned to spring, there was more good news as Fritz was given a more suitable residence in Berlin; and, in the summer, he moved his little family to what was to become their favourite home: the New Palace in Potsdam.

"Long shady avenues stretched out from the Palace in every direction," wrote Vicky's lady-in-waiting. "The Princess and I used to walk there in the moonlit summer evenings when everybody had gone to bed, and lie in wait behind a hedge or a tree to try and frighten the Prince, who still would continue his nocturnal perambulations."[83]

Fritz and Vicky were free to decorate the palace according to their own taste; and to design the gardens, which they placed under the direction of an Englishman, Walker, who regularly gave guests tours of the estate. Indoors, there were music rooms, and a disused theatre, where Voltaire had once directed his plays, and which

---

[g] The Landtag was the Prussian parliament, which comprised two Chambers: the elected Lower Chamber or House of Representatives; and the Upper Chamber or House of Lords (*Herrenhaus*).

Vicky transformed into an art studio where she could indulge her passion – and considerable talent – for painting. Fritz was so proud of her work that he always made a point of directing guests to the studio because, as one visitor recorded, 'he was determined that we should see, and duly admire, his wife's artistic talents.'[84]

His own rooms were decorated with photographs and paintings of military leaders and famous battles; while the immense empty attic, which ran the entire length of the building, would become a perfect indoor playground, gymnasium and dancing school for his children.

The New Palace became a centre of culture as the couple entertained artists, composers, scientists and men of learning. From there, too, Vicky planned and executed her many philanthropic schemes, which, over the years, would include establishing temporary work and training programmes for the unemployed; lessons in health and hygiene for women and for the poor; schools of nursing; and an institute for young women to learn a trade.

In spite of the splendour of their surroundings, the Hohenzollerns' legendary frugality prevailed within the palace walls. Fritz frequently complained that his allowance was insufficient to meet his needs and, consequently, he and Vicky lived very simply. A visitor, who had been invited to join them for dinner, was surprised when he entered a grand, ornate dining room, to find that, rather than the great banquet that he had anticipated, Fritz and Vicky shared a table with one equerry and one lady-in-waiting. The meal consisted solely of 'curds and whey, veal cutlets, and a rice pudding. Nothing else whatever'[85]; and, afterwards, Vicky herself served the men tankards of beer.

Chapter 7 – From God's Hand and From None Other

In October 1858, Queen Elizabeth finally resigned herself to the truth that the King would never recover, and, with great reluctance she agreed that, rather than renewing a temporary regency, Prince William's position should be made permanent. The news was greeted with resignation rather than enthusiasm, as the liberals remembered how heavy-handedly William had crushed the 1848 revolution; and the pro-Russian ministers feared his attachment to Britain.

To appease the liberals, the Prince dismissed his brother's reactionary government, replacing the Minister President, Otto Theodore von Manteuffel, with two liberal-minded ministers: his old friend, the Roman Catholic Prince Karl Anton of Hohenzollern-Sigmaringen; and Baron Rudolf von Auerswald. He asserted, too, that he was committed to the constitution and promised that, on his accession, he would swear an oath to uphold it.

This, however, was merely an experiment in liberalism, for, although he was keen to distance himself from his brother's autocracy, he was equally determined to protect the privileges of the Crown. For the most part, his advisors were reactionaries and, when the elections returned a higher number of progressives, he stated firmly that he 'never could permit the progressive development of the nation's inner political life to question or endanger the rights of the Crown or the power of Prussia.'[86] Above all, he refused to allow the progressives to hinder his plans for an increase in military spending, as the army was too small and too ill-equipped to defend the kingdom if Prussia were suddenly dragged into a war.

He had not forgotten the French invasion of Berlin, or his father's humiliation at having to yield to Napoleon's terms; and when the French Emperor Napoleon III – a nephew of Napoleon Bonaparte – formed an alliance with Sardinia, the Regent feared that he intended to repeat his uncle's military conquests.

At that time, Italy, like Germany, was a conglomeration of separate states, several of which were dominated by Austria. The Sardinians had long been seeking independence, and, in 1859, having secured Napoleon III's support, they felt powerful enough to provoke the Austrians into a declaration of war.

This left Prince William in a difficult position. A Sardinian victory would weaken Austria, which would strengthen Prussia; but, equally, it could encourage Napoleon III's dreams of expansion and propel him into invading the Rhineland.

The situation could not have developed at a more inopportune moment, as the Prussian ministers were so new to their roles that they had not had time to decide their specific duties or to learn how to govern. The ministry was, as one British diplomat reported:

"...composed of the most heterogeneous elements, hardly acquainted with each other and wholly unfamiliar with the higher management of public affairs, had taken office, not as an organised political party, disciplined by a successful opposition, but as the personal friends of a prince whose position, until the advent of the Regency, had necessarily been a passive one, and were bound to each other by no more positive ties than those of a common appreciation...of the political rottenness to which their predecessors had been in a fairway of reducing the State, joined to an honest desire to remedy the harm already done."[87]

To make matters worse, a rumour spread that the British were about to enter the conflict in support of the Sardinians and French. As Vicky desperately urged her mother to maintain British neutrality, Fritz was becoming exasperated by his father's inaction, which gave the impression of Prussian weakness.

The French and Sardinians stormed through Italy, achieving victory after victory, and finally, Prince William, fearing an invasion, ordered a partial mobilisation along the Prussian border. Fritz was promoted to the command of the 1st Infantry Division of Guards, and told to prepare his troops for battle. Such a wave of patriotism swept through the kingdom that even Vicky became excited at the prospect of a victorious war. To her mother, she wrote of her hope that:

"...we will soon be engaged – and pass the Rhine – the sooner the better – and by a successful war obtain for us a lasting and honourable peace, secure our position as the first in Germany and help the Austrians by helping ourselves and make for ourselves a great political position."[88]

In the event, the Prussians arrived too late to take part in the conflict, as, following a victory at Solferino, Napoleon III arranged to discuss peace terms with the Austrian Emperor, Franz Josef. It was widely reported that Napoleon was eager to end the war because he was so disgusted by the slaughter at Solferino, but he later admitted that, on the morning of the battle, his wife had sent word that the Prussians were advancing and he feared that they intended to invade France.

In fact, as Fritz and his father knew, the Prussian regiments were not fit to launch an invasion; and the war had merely highlighted the inadequacy of their armed forces. Significantly smaller than those of the other German states, the standing army was chiefly made up of conscripts, forty-thousands of whom were enlisted annually to serve for three years before entering the reserve – the *Landwehr* – for a further two years. At any one time, approximately two-hundred-thousand men were available for service, whereas other states had more than double that number. To reduce the difference, the period of reserve was extended to seven years but it soon became clear that this was wholly impracticable. At a moment's notice, the *Landwehrmen* could be called away from their families, farms and workshops and so they lived in a constant state of uncertainty. Having settled into civilian life, many were so reluctant return to active service that, if they were forced to do so, they lacked the enthusiasm and patriotism required to secure victories.

To rectify this, the Regent planned to increase the number of conscripts to sixty-three-thousand per year, and to lengthen the period of service to establish a larger standing army. This would ensure that the *Landwehrmen* would only be called up in extreme circumstances and, even then, they would be restricted to non-combatant duties.

Fritz fully supported his father's plan, but the Landtag, with its progressive majority, refused to release the necessary funding. The Junkers[h], who resented the Regent's promise to adhere to the constitution, were equally obstructive, and the secretly planned to use his failure to pass his military reforms to force him to abdicate in favour of his son.

In the autumn of 1859, as his father was being buffeted by the political storm, Fritz was being hurled about by the choppy waves of the English Channel. He and Vicky were travelling to Windsor for the Prince of Wales' eighteenth birthday, but the sea was so rough that they were both terribly sea-sick. Grateful to reach land, they took several hours to recover, but, happily, by the time they arrived in Windsor on 8th November, they were well enough to respond to the resounding cheers of the crowds.

Bells rang and a Guard of Honour lined the route to the Castle, where Queen Victoria eagerly awaited a joyful

---

[h] Junkers were the landed gentry or minor nobility.

reunion and an opportunity to delve into the state of her daughter's marriage. While Fritz went shooting with Prince Albert, and toured the Portsmouth shipyards, the Queen plied Vicky's companion, 'Lena' – Countess Madeleine Blucher – with questions about the couple's life in Prussia. Lena's responses and her own observations reassured her that all was well, and her only disappointment was that they had not brought baby William with them.

Prince Albert noted that they both had matured since their wedding, and that Vicky had 'made great progress…in knowledge of the world.'

> "I was delighted," he wrote to Princess Augusta when the couple returned to Prussia, "to find in Fritz so much more frankness and self-confidence, and a far wider intellectual horizon. Many of the books of life lie open to him which before were closed. Vicky has become more sensible and precise-thinking, and has already collected a great deal of experience."[89]

While Fritz had been enjoying his English holiday, his father's dispute with the Landtag had continued unabated. Unwilling to take any drastic measures while serving only as regent, he believed that he would be in a far more powerful position once he became king. By the summer of 1860, it seemed that he would not have long to wait as Frederick William's condition had significantly deteriorated.

> "I never saw so lamentable an object," Vicky wrote to Queen Victoria. "…He was lying in his bath chair his left hand and arm which he has quite lost the use of as well as both his legs tied up in cloths…he can neither speak nor look at anyone as he has lost the power of directing his eyes…you never saw anything so sad."[90]

He lingered in the same abject state for a further six months until New Year's Eve 1860, when the Regent, while dining with Fritz and Vicky, received a telegram telling him that his brother's condition had worsened. Not unduly alarmed, he set out for the Sansoucci Palace, telling Fritz that he would send for him if necessary. Fritz returned home and went to bed but, soon after midnight, he was woken by an urgent message from the Sansoucci, telling him to come at once as the King was dying. Throughout the whole of the following day and night, he remained at Frederick William's bedside until, on 2nd January, his uncle finally slipped away. In keeping with the Prussian tradition, the obsequies were completed quickly, and, at his own request, the late King's heart was removed from his body to be interred with his parents in the Charlottenburg Mausoleum, while the rest of his remains were buried in Friedenskirche in Potsdam.

Throughout the reign of Frederick William IV, Fritz had watched the kingdom sink from revolution into apathy, until Prussia appeared to be nothing more than a minor state caught between two mighty empires. His father, now King William, had the desire and opportunity to inject a new dynamism into domestic and foreign affairs and, with his planned military and political reforms, he could establish Prussia's position as a major European power.

"The new King," wrote Princess Radziwill, "…was ambitious to a degree that no one who had known him previous to his coming to the throne had ever suspected."[91]

Within days of his brother's funeral, the King demonstrated his commitment to the army by presenting the colours to the regiments that he had established during the regency. More controversially, he asserted his authority by stating that he would be crowned in a spectacular ceremony. His disconcerted ministers reminded him that his predecessors had foregone an expensive coronation and had instead made donations to projects that would benefit the public. The King not only ignored their protestations but went much further by insisting that he would be crowned in Konigsberg – the location of the coronation of the first Prussian King, Frederick I – thereby demonstrating his belief in the hereditary right of kings. Moreover, the oaths of allegiance, which were usually sworn in private, would take place in public during the ceremony.

The dispute between the King and his advisors continued for several months and, in July, when Fritz went to Osborne with Vicky, he discussed the situation with Prince Albert. After much reflection, he wrote a tactful letter to his father, suggesting that he could pay a formal visit to Konigsberg to show his respect for ancient traditions, followed by a coronation in Berlin, which would demonstrate his commitment to a more modern monarchy. He showed the letter to Prince Albert, who approved of the recommendation but was shocked when Fritz added a paragraph stressing the necessity of showing the authority of the Crown to counteract the concessions granted in the 1848 revolution. Prince Albert urged him to alter the paragraph or to remove it altogether, but Fritz ignored his advice, insisting that he believed what he had written.

A few days later, on 14th July, the dispute about the coronation might have become immaterial, as the King, who was visiting Baden-Baden, was the target of a would-be assassin. Oskar Becker, a native of Odessa and student at Leipzig University, walked up behind him and discharged two bullets from a pistol. Amazingly, but for a bruise on his back, King William escaped uninjured; and Becker was arrested at the scene and subsequently sentenced to twenty years in prison[i].

Neither the assassination attempt nor Fritz' letter could persuade the King to change his mind about the Konigsberg coronation; and, in late September, he arrived

---

[i] At the King's request, Becker was released from prison five years later and his sentence was commuted to exile for life.

in the city to take personal charge of the final preparations. The ceremony took place in the chapel of Kongsberg Castle, on 18th October 1861 – Fritz' thirtieth birthday – and, in spite of his initial reservations, Fritz was 'in a great state of emotion and excitement'[92] at the prospect of playing his part in such a momentous event. He was, however, as surprised as the rest of the congregation when, in a gesture worthy of Napoleon, his father took the crown from the altar and placed it on his own head, stating: 'I receive this from God's hand and from none other.'

"The speeches of the King of Prussia at Konigsberg have produced a bad impression here," Prince Albert wrote to Baron Stockmar, "and the theory of the Divine right of kings (apart from being an absurdity in itself, and exploded here for the last two hundred years) is suitable neither to the position and vocation of Prussia nor to those of the King. The difficulty of establishing united action between Prussia and England has been again infinitely augmented by this royal programme."[93]

The London *Times,* which constantly criticised Prussia, condemned the King with such vehemence that, when the reports were printed in Berlin, they created a wave of anti-British feeling. Even the Prussian liberals were so incensed that they defended the King's actions; and the majority of his people praised him for showing such strength of character. Three days later, when he returned to Berlin, huge crowds turned out to welcome him, prompting one witness to note that 'the reception was like that given to a victorious soldier after a great battle.'[94] The glorious sunshine shimmering on his ceremonial sword, Fritz proudly rode beside his father, behind columns of guildsmen and soldiers, followed by the Queen and princesses in a series of gilded glass coaches. 'The universal enthusiasm carried one away,' recorded one observer. 'There was such genuine and hearty devotion.'[95]

"The King of Prussia," wrote a British politician who had attended the coronation, "has before him one of the most glorious enterprises monarch ever undertook. If he had a little more of his ancestor Frederic and less of his brother Frederic William, he would be at the head of Germany in less than two years…I should like to be in his place."[96]

The future looked bright for King William and his dynasty.

Chapter 8 – In a State of Passive Neutrality

The excitement of the coronation had barely faded when Vicky received a letter from her mother, telling her that Prince Albert was suffering from a cold with neuralgia. Recently, said the Queen, his gloom and depression had been exacerbated by insomnia, but she was sure that he would soon recover as he had been similarly afflicted the previous winter. She did not mention that for several months he had complained of a myriad of ailments, from abscesses on his gums to severe rheumatic spasms and a worsening of his chronic digestive disorders. Over the next few days, further letters reported that he was confined to bed with a fever, but, as Queen Victoria fluctuated between hope and fear, she described every minor improvement as a sign of his imminent recovery.

Prince Albert, however, was convinced that he was dying, and, on 4th December 1861, he asked his second daughter, Alice, to warn her elder sister to prepare herself for the worst. Horrified and distraught, Vicky yearned to go at once to Windsor, but the King and the court doctors refused to allow her to leave. She was again pregnant, and the doctors warned that it was not safe for her to travel, but there was also the fear that, if her father had a fever, she could contract an infection and bring it back to Berlin.

Throughout the following week, letters flew back and forth between England and Prussia, and, although her anxiety had not lessened, Vicky was led to believe that her father remained stable. Not until 12th December, when his mind began to wander, did Queen Victoria admit that her forty-two-year-old husband was dying.

Fritz received the dreaded telegram in the morning of 15th December, informing him that Prince Albert had died shortly before eleven o'clock the previous night, and it was now his responsibility to break the tragic news to Vicky.

'Oh, why does the earth not swallow me up!' she gasped; and, for several weeks, she frequently broke down in tears. Even six months later, she sighed that she could never be happy again, and her only solace was the thought of returning to England as soon as possible. Fritz did his utmost to ease her grief, as her lady-in-waiting observed:

> "She certainly has the kindest and most devoted of nurses (I may almost say) in the excellent Crown Prince, who seems to think of nothing else but how to try to alleviate her sorrow."[97]

While caring for his wife, and genuinely grieving the loss of a friend and mentor, Fritz was also becoming increasingly concerned about his father, whose acrimonious dispute with the Landtag showed no sign of reaching a satisfactory conclusion. In September 1862, the Landtag devoted five days to discussing the military budget, and the outcome was even worse than the King had expected. Not only had the funding for the army been refused but also the budget was backdated, which meant that the regiments that he had established during the regency would have to be disbanded.

The next day, the King summoned his ministers and set out three possible options: he could yield to the Landtag, which was too great a humiliation; he could dissolve parliament, which might lead to civil war; or he could abdicate in favour of his son. His ministers urged him to endure the humiliation and accept the Landtag's decision but instead he prepared a notice of abdication.

Aghast at so drastic an action, the Minister of War, Albert von Roon, suggested an alternative solution: the King could summon Bismarck to Berlin, and appoint him as his Chief Minister. Roon assured him that the highly-gifted Bismarck was the only man with sufficient skill and strength to force the Landtag into line and to ensure that the army reforms were enacted. He would stop at nothing to achieve his ends, and, although he had a reputation for underhand dealings, he was also an ardent patriot and committed to the service of the Crown. The King was no more impressed by this idea than by any of the other suggestions, for, while he acknowledged that Bismarck was a gifted statesman, he had serious doubts about his unscrupulous methods.

Ambitious for himself and for Prussia, forty-seven-year-old Bismarck's greatest assets were his patience, resolve and careful calculations. Once he had set his mind to a plan, he never acted on impulse but, like a Grand Master in a chess game, he carefully considered every possible outcome to ensure that he would outwit his opponents. Gouty, often grumpy and moody, he cleverly set his enemies against one another, and ruthlessly destroyed their careers by leaking actual or fabricated scandals to the press.

Like his father, Fritz admired Bismarck's abilities and his loyalty to the Crown, but he worried about his methods and his known disdain for Britain. In the middle of the crisis, Fritz took Vicky to Coburg to meet Queen Victoria, who remarked that Bismarck was 'a very bad man' and it would be better for the King to abdicate than to appoint him. Vicky agreed with her assessment of the statesman but warned that it would be dangerous for Fritz to encourage his father to abdicate as it could give the impression that he was trying to seize the crown, which would damage his reputation for the rest of his reign. Fritz himself was more alarmed than excited by the thought of assuming power at a time of such contention between the monarchy and the Landtag – an opinion shared by his advisors, who warned him to avoid any involvement in the dispute.

On 18th September, when the King summoned him to Potsdam to discuss the situation, Fritz advised him neither to abdicate nor to appoint Bismarck but he was unable to suggest an alternative solution. When Fritz had gone, the desperate King turned again to the War Minister, Roon, who reiterated that Bismarck was the only man who could resolve the dispute with the Landtag. This time, the King reluctantly agreed to summon the statesman to Potsdam.

As soon as Fritz heard that Bismarck was approaching, he sent him a telegram summoning him to a meeting before he visited the King. He arrived at the New Palace on 20th September but was determinedly unforthcoming, refusing to speak of his plans until he had spoken with Fritz' father. Instead, he complained of how badly he had been treated, having been told to expect a summons and then left for many months in a state of limbo.

"The cause of my vexation," he wrote later, "was the King's having led me to believe that in six weeks at the latest he would come to a decision about my future – i.e. whether I was to take up my residence in Berlin, Paris, or London – that a quarter of a year had already passed away, and that autumn was come before I knew where I was to spend the winter."[98]

King William was most put out when he heard of Bismarck's meeting with Fritz, suspecting that he had heard of his threat to abdicate and had been trying to curry favour with his successor. When they met at Babelsberg two days later, the King accused him directly of plotting with his son but Bismarck adamantly denied the charge before stating in the starkest terms that they now faced a choice between monarchical or parliamentary governance. The latter, he said, would prevent Prussia from attaining her rightful place in the world and leave all the German states under Austrian domination.

More concerned with military spending than with Bismarck's wider vision, the King asked if he would be able to form a government that was sufficiently powerful to enact his reforms. Once Bismarck had given that assurance, the King appointed him as provisional Minister President, and told him to set about forming a Cabinet.

Eight days later, Bismarck set out his vision to the Budget Committee of the Landtag:

"The position of Prussia in Germany will not be determined by its liberalism but by its power...Not through speeches and majority decisions will the great questions of the day be decided – that was the great mistake of 1848 and 1849 – but by blood and iron."[99]

His belligerent tone not only alarmed the liberals in the Landtag, but also shocked the kings of the other German states, who feared that he intended to force them into subservience to Prussia. Fritz, too, was left in an awkward position, as he could not speak out against the Minister President for fear of offending his father, but his silence disappointed and irked the progressives who had been looking to him for support. Criticised by his former supporters, Fritz was happy to escape from Berlin by embarking on a tour of Italy with Vicky and her brother, Bertie, the Prince of Wales.

In spite of his initial misgivings, Fritz was not entirely uncomfortable with Bismarck's appointment; and he was happily surprised that, during his Italian tour, the Minister President kept him informed of all the political developments. From Naples, his aide-de-camp wrote to Bismarck on his behalf:

"The Crown Prince, who is accustomed to being ignored or slighted by his uncles, and especially by the late King's highest officials, appreciates your attentions; your first letter, which I brought, and still more the sending of a courier, have pleased him very much."[100]

During Fritz' absence, Bismarck set in motion an ingenious plan to obtain the necessary funding for the

---

[j] The term combined the roles of Foreign Minister and President; and five months later, the position was made permanent.

King's military reforms. By law, a budget could only come into effect when it had been agreed by the Upper and Lower Chambers of the Landtag, so Bismarck cleverly engineered a dispute between the two Chambers to prevent the budget from being enacted. He then twisted the wording of the constitution to declare that, in the absence of a functioning government, the Crown had the right and duty to take charge of public spending. The military funding was secured; the King was delighted; and Bismarck, who had achieved in weeks what the King had failed to achieve in months, knew that his powerful position was secured.

By the time that Fritz returned to Berlin in mid-December, a new and more confident spirit pervaded the city and the army; and, in spite of Vicky's warnings that the 'very bad man' intended to destroy the constitution, Fritz could not disguise his satisfaction that he had brought the dispute between the King and the Landtag to a successful conclusion. Within a month, however, Fritz was shocked by Bismarck's first foray into foreign policy, which almost brought Prussia to the brink of war.

In January 1863, when the Poles staged an uprising against Russian rule, Bismarck, feared that, if they gained independence, they could threaten parts of East Prussia. He hastily dispatched four military corps to the border, and made arrangements with the Tsar to work together to suppress the rebellion. Sympathetic to the Poles, Napoleon III called on Britain and Austria to join him in an anti-Russian alliance, prompting Fritz to ask Vicky to plead with her mother to maintain British neutrality.

This time, however, Bismarck failed to obtain the support that he had expected, as many ordinary Prussians, sympathised with the Poles; and the King, determined to avoid his late brother's reliance on Russia, was unenthusiastic about the military arrangements. Ultimately, the Russians suppressed the uprising without Prussian assistance, but the incident deepened the growing schism between Bismarck and his Cabinet, and the Landtag.

Tensions between the ministers and members were never more apparent than when Bismarck appeared in the Lower Chamber. As a minister, he had the right to address the members, but he objected to the fact that the members also had a right to interrupt him. He 'could not bear to have anyone inferior to himself meddling with his action…Even at the beginning of his ministerial career, when he had just assumed the direction of public affairs, he had felt impatient with the people with whom he found himself compelled to associate.'[101]

While he was giving a lengthy speech about the situation in Poland, the President of the Chamber stood up to complain that he had digressed from the original topic. 'I am not subject to the disciplinary power of the Chamber,' he retorted angrily. '…I have one superior only, his Majesty the King.'[102]

A few days later, when the War Minister, Roon, was likewise interrupted, he declared that if such behaviour continued, ministers would no longer attend the Chamber. On being informed of the dispute, the King sided firmly with Roon, and sent a message to the Landtag:

> "The Ministers enjoy my confidence, and their actions have my sanction. I thank them for opposing the unconstitutional aggression of the Chamber."[103]

Later that day, in response to the ministers' complaints, the King went further and prorogued parliament.

For Bismarck this was the triumph of monarchical over parliamentary governance that had been the condition on which he accepted his position; but for Fritz it was a blatant disregard for the constitution. His supporters and members of the Landtag again urged him to speak out against the Minister President, but instead he assured his father that he would never publicly criticise his policies.

"I am silent, and live in a state of passive neutrality," he wrote sadly to a friend. "I shall neither achieve nor prevent anything, as everything is the direct outcome of circumstances which have been deliberately created and brought to pass."[104]

As he had suspected, the prorogation of the Landtag was only the beginning of Bismarck's seizure of power; but, bound by his promise to his father, he watched in silence as, through various underhand schemes, the Minister President gradually took control of every major institution. Through a network of spies, he discovered exactly who opposed him and, through his contacts in the press, he was free to employ his usual method of destroying his critics' careers and reputations.

His spies, operating even within the New Palace, brought him 'disturbing' reports that large sections of the public believed that the King would die soon, and his popular successor would introduce a more democratic constitution. 'The pernicious prejudice' he was told, had to be eradicated for fear that it could lead to the King's assassination. The only solution was to force Fritz to 'decisively and publicly declare that he is in complete accord with the King's political principles.'[105]

Fritz was torn between those who were urging him to express his support for the King; and Vicky and his friends, who advised him to distance himself from his father, whose dependence on Bismarck, was damaging to the kingdom. He remained determinedly silent, quietly continuing his military duties, and avoided making any political statements. In May 1863, however, he was shocked when he arrived in East Prussia to review the troops to discover that no crowds had turned out to welcome him, and the customary loyal addresses were notable for their absence. Fearing that, in East Prussia at least, the King had lost the support of his people, he wrote to his father, urging him to adopt a different course and not to 'infringe the law' by overriding the constitution.

The next day, he was horrified to discover that the official Crown publication contained an ordinance imposing censorship on the press. Offended that he had not been consulted about the decision, he wrote to Bismarck in the strongest terms, stating that the ordinance was illegal and that he wished to dissociate himself from it. Four days later, as Bismarck had not even bothered to reply to his letter, he wrote again to his father; and, that evening, while addressing the leading citizens of Danzig, he made no attempt to conceal his true opinion. Although he was careful to speak in only the highest terms of the King, he made it clear that he had not been party to the ordinance, leaving his hearers in no doubt that he opposed it.

The press published the speech in full, creating a sensation; and the liberals who had seen Fritz' silence as a sign of weakness, now hailed him as their champion. A few days later, their admiration increased when his private letters to his father, criticising the ministry, were leaked to a leading Berlin newspaper. The British press took up the story, and heaped praise on his the 'brave' Crown Prince, leaving Bismarck and his fellow ministers convinced that Vicky was responsible for his 'unpatriotic act' and 'disobedience.'

The furious King wrote him an angry letter, berating him as though he were a child, and threatening to dismiss him from all his civic and military duties unless he retracted his speech in an open letter to the press.

Utterly distraught, Fritz:

"...sat up till one last night, writing the answer...in which [he] says that he is almost broken-hearted at causing his father so much pain, but that he could not retract the words spoken...at Danzig; that he had always hoped the King's Government would not act in a way which should force him to put himself in direct opposition to the King; but now it had come to that, and he (Fritz) would stand by his opinions. He felt that under such circumstances it would be impossible for him to retain any office military or civil, and he laid both at the feet of the King."[106]

The more reactionary ministers urged the King to strip him of his military rank, while others said that he ought to be banished to a remote castle, and his English wife should be sent into exile.

Only the wily Bismarck understood that any obvious punishment would increase Fritz' popularity and make him the focal point for any opposition to the King. Instead, the arch-manipulator devised the far less conspicuous but equally cruel punishment of slowly wearing him down by excluding him from affairs of state and compelling him to fill his time with tiring but trivial duties.

Chapter 9 – Successful Villainy

In March 1863, Vicky's brother, Bertie, married the beautiful Alexandra of Denmark, a daughter of the heir to the Danish throne. Eight months later, her father succeeded as King Christian IX, and one of his first acts was to sign a constitution, incorporating the duchy of Holstein into Denmark. This move provoked widespread indignation in Berlin, as the Elbe duchies of Schleswig and Holstein had long been the focus of a bitter dispute between Denmark and Prussia. The background to the squabble was so complex that, as the British Prime Minister, Palmerston, remarked, only three people had ever understood it: Prince Albert, who was dead; a German professor, who had gone insane; and himself, and he had forgotten it.

While feigning outrage, Bismarck privately relished King Christian's 'illegal' actions as they provided an ideal excuse for a war in which the Danes could be portrayed as the aggressors. Victory would not only ignite a sense of Prussian patriotism but would also bring commercial gains to the kingdom. As foreign ships paid heavy tolls to pass through the Danish straits, the Germans and Austrians had long envisaged a canal in Kiel to gain direct access to the North Sea and the Baltic. Kiel, however, was situated in Danish-controlled Holstein, and so, when the Austrian Emperor heard that the Prussians were considering seizing the duchy, he offered to send a couple of regiments to support the invasion.

Fritz was equally outraged by King's Christian's constitution, as he believed the Elbe duchies should be granted autonomy under Duke Frederick of Schleswig-Holstein-Sonderburg-Augustenburg, with whom he had struck up a friendship during his student days in Bonn. The Duke, a German of Danish descent, had arguably the most solid claim to the region and had not only won the support of many German liberals but also had the tacit backing of the King. Bismarck, however, intended to annex the duchies for Prussia, and dismissed Fritz' idea in a letter to a colleague:

> "Of all the policies we could follow, the most inept would be for Prussia to cooperate to establish a new German Grand Duchy, to create a Prince who, in time of peace will vote against us...and in time of war would compromise us if he does not betray us."[107]

In January 1864, Bismarck sent King Christian an ultimatum: unless he withdrew his claim to Holstein, he would find himself at war with Austria and Prussia. The panicking Princess of Wales pleaded with the British Government to provide military support for her father; and the British press, supported by the maverick Prime Minister, Palmerston, was filled with anti-Prussian, pro-Danish headlines.

Irked by the insults, and believing that Vicky was passing military secrets to her mother, Bismarck warned the King that she had too great an influence over her husband, who, therefore, could not be trusted. The King responded by ordering Fritz to refrain from discussing military or political matters with Vicky, as she could be a threat to national security.

In fact, from the moment that war broke out both Fritz and Vicky wholeheartedly committed themselves to the service of the country. As Fritz set out to Holstein with his regiment, Vicky complained bitterly to Queen Victoria about the anti-Prussian propaganda in the British press and parliament.

> "The highly pathetic, philanthropic and virtuous tone in which all the attacks against Prussia are made, has something intensely ridiculous about it," she wrote. "The English would not like it if they were engaged in a war, to be dictated to in a pompous style, how they were to conduct it, indeed

I am sure they would not stand such interference. Why should we then be supposed to submit to it?"[108]

Her younger sister, Alice, who was also living in Germany, having recently married the heir to the Grand Duchy of Hesse-Darmstadt, was equally indignant about the negative reports in the British press. Telling her mother that the Prussians were freeing the people of Holstein from the 'Danish yoke', she asked why England was trying to prevent them from escaping from oppression.

The Prince and Princess of Wales, though, continued to plead for support for the Danes until Queen Victoria, annoyed by the constant bickering, forbade any further mention of Schleswig-Holstein; and when she heard the bellicose speeches of the gung-ho Palmerston, she let it be known that she would never sanction Britain's entry into the conflict.

"The Queen is so set against the war," Sir Stafford Northcote reported, "that…I should think she would rather dismiss her Ministry…than give in."[109]

Queen Sophie of the Netherlands was more outspoken in her criticism of the Prussians, accusing them of being 'strong in their violent pretensions; but it is no easy matter to give to understand to a people, who wishes to become a nation, that whatever they claim or urge is wrong and folly.'[110]

While the debates continued, Fritz was steadily approaching Kiel, his progress hindered more by the poor state of the roads than by Danish resistance. His men were impressed by his willingness to share their hardships and the cheerful manner with which he moved among them. He dutifully kept Bismarck informed of the regiment's position and he used his experience to offer him advice about military strategy. When, however, Bismarck asked him about the Holsteiners' reaction to the prospect of living under Prussian rule, he curtly pointed out that he could not comment on such a matter as he had not been consulted about the statesman's objectives.

> "I regret that I am unable to give you my support in respect of the political side of the question you have addressed to me, as I am unacquainted with the aims of our policy."[111]

In Jutland, the Danes suffered a series of defeats and, by April 1864, only eight weeks after the outbreak of war, they were so disheartened that they agreed to an armistice. The following month, the British Foreign Secretary, Lord John Russell, presided over a peace conference in London at which the majority of delegates agreed that the duchies should become autonomous and governed by the Duke of Augustenburg. Delighted, Fritz invited his old friend to Berlin, telling him that:

> "Bismarck himself said to me yesterday that now England and Austria are for you (France has been inclined that way for some time) and that therefore the moment has come to negotiate with you directly."[112]

On 1st June, crowds welcomed the Duke to Berlin, and King William was so pleased to see him that he wrote to his mother to tell her that the duchies would undoubtedly be granted to her son. Bismarck, however, had not lost sight of his annexation plans and, following a three-hour meeting with the Duke, he informed the King that he had refused to accept certain conditions and, therefore, it would be impossible to support him. To a friend, he wrote more bluntly that 'it is not for a nobody like the Prince of Augustenburg that Prussia is spending the blood of its soldiers and the money of its treasury.'[113]

After two months, the London Peace Conference ended in stalemate, and hostilities briefly resumed until King Christian was forced into an unconditional surrender. Further anti-Prussian articles appeared in the British press, several of which implied that Fritz was of the same mind as

Bismarck. 'The feeling against us now in England is most unjust!' Vicky exclaimed before decrying the British Ambassador for failing to present a more accurate picture of what was happening. It was left to the British diplomat, Robert Morier, to assure his government that Fritz was unimpressed by the Minister President:

> "I had upon my return to Berlin some long and interesting conversations both with the Crown Prince and Crown Princess. To my very great satisfaction I found that the supposed brilliancy of Bismarck's successes during the last four months had altogether failed to produce any impression upon them, except the deep disgust which well-ordered minds feel at successful villainy."[114]

This did not ease the resentment felt by the Prince and Princess of Wales, and, when they paid a fleeting visit to Prussia the following autumn, the Prince was most put out during his brief meetings with his brother-in-law because, 'it was not pleasant to see him and his A.D.C. always in Prussian uniform flaunting before our eyes a most objectionable ribbon which he received for his deeds of valour??? against the unhappy Danes.'[115]

Bismarck was also put out when the peace negotiations concluded with the Treaty of Vienna, which awarded Prussia and Austria joint control of the Elbe duchies. As the Austrians had played only a minor role in the conflict, Bismarck asked Emperor Franz Josef to give Prussia a greater share of the spoils, and, when his request was ignored, he was more determined than ever to crush his erstwhile ally.

At that time, Fritz was more concerned with the welfare of the soldiers than with Bismarck's political intrigues, as the campaign had exposed the problems caused by inappropriate uniforms and a lack of suitable equipment. Determined to resolve the issues before any future conflict, he informed the Minister of War and the

Commander-in-Chief of the Armed Forces that the infantry's tunics were so tight that they restricted the soldiers' movement. As his recommendations were ignored, he decided to demonstrate his point while inspecting the troops in front of a number of senior officers. As he walked along the line, he dropped a gold coin onto the ground and said any man who picked it up could keep it, but, when those nearest to him attempted to do so, their belts and tunics prevented them from bending.

"And how," Fritz asked, "do you expect to win battles with soldiers hampered to such an extent as that in their movements? What greater demonstration than this is needed to prove the justice of my argument?"[116]

The resentful officers, reported the incident to the Minister of War, who informed the King that his son's behaviour was tantamount to insubordination. Then, said his father, he must accept the prescribed punishment for the offence, and sentenced him to temporary house arrest in a distant castle.

The ink was barely dry on the Treaty of Vienna before the inadequacy of the new arrangements came to light. Having little interest in the duchies, the Austrians reverted to the earlier suggestion of granting Schleswig-Holstein autonomy within the German Confederation[k], under the direction of the Duke of Augustenburg. Bismarck was so incensed that he declared that annexation was the only solution; and, during a meeting of the Council of Ministers in May 1865, the majority of the ministers agreed. Fritz alone warned that this would damage Prussia's reputation, and he reiterated his belief that the Duke of Augustenburg was the only ruler who would be

---

[k] The German Confederation was a collection of German-speaking states, loosely modelled on the former Holy Roman Empire.

accepted by all parties. Bismarck ignored his argument and, three months later, the Duke's claim was declared illegal.

Unbeknown to Fritz, Bismarck had entered into secret negotiations with his Austrian counterpart, Gustav von Blome, with whom he arranged a meeting between King William and Emperor Franz Josef in the Alpine resort of Bad Gastein. Determined to prevent Fritz from influencing the discussions, Bismarck warned the King not to mention the plan to his son, for fear that he would tell his wife, who in turn would tell the rulers of the smaller German states, which would jeopardise the negotiations and could provoke an Austro-Prussian War.

The clandestine summit took place on 14th August, and resulted in the 'Gastein Convention.' Both parties agreed that the they would retain joint control of the duchies but the Prussians would take over the administration of Schleswig, and the Austrians that of Holstein. To enable the Prussians to access Schleswig, they were guaranteed free passage through Holstein; and a financial settlement was arranged to enable King William to purchase the duchy of Lauenburg from Austria.

Three days later, on being told of the new arrangements, Fritz was appalled, knowing that the Gastein Convention was merely a ruse designed by Bismarck to enable him to annex the duchies. The British and the smaller German states were equally aghast; and even the Prussian Treasury objected to the cost of purchasing Lauenburg[1].

Within two months of the meeting at Bad Gastein, Bismarck complained that the Austrians were continuing to promote the claims of Duke of Augustenburg; and, in January 1866, he sent an indignant message to Vienna, objecting to the rise of anti-Prussian feeling in Holstein, and accusing the Austrians of allowing revolutionary

---

[1] In fact, King William paid for Lauenburg from his own funds.

activity in the duchies. Again, presenting Prussia as the innocent party, he warned that unless the Austrians quashed the dissention, King William would be forced to abandon all previous agreements.

This was precisely what Fritz had predicted would happen, and when the Austrians sent a vague reply, he knew that Bismarck was deliberately creating an excuse for war. A few days later, when the Council of Ministers discussed making war preparations, Fritz was the only member to vote against the motion.

"Nobody knows better than I do that my opinions are of no weight;" he confided in a friend, "but I was bound at least to show that I did not regard the projected conflict as unavoidable."[117]

When Franz Josef became aware of the Prussian military preparations, he sent troops towards the border and hastily sought assurances from the southern German states that, in the event of a conflict, they would side with Austria.

Fritz was alarmed by the prospect of war, not only because he feared that Prussia might be defeated but also because he knew that it would divide his extended family. His sister's duchy of Baden was allied to Austria, as was Hesse-Darmstadt, the adopted home of Vicky's sister, Alice.

"We are living in such a state of anxiety and alarm," Alice wrote to Queen Victoria. "War would be too fearful a thing to contemplate – brother against brother, friend against friend, as it will be in this case!"[118]

Disgusted by Bismarck's intrigues, Fritz was even more appalled by his blatant refusal to consider a peaceful solution.

"We are still midway between peace and war;" Vicky wrote to her mother, "not a day passes without some little incident which might be easily laid hold of to turn the scaled on the side of peace, and not a day passes that the wicked man does not with the greatest ability counteract and thwart what is good, and drive on towards war, turning and twisting everything to serve his own purpose."[119]

In April 1866, the Italians let it be known that, if war broke out within three months, they would also declare war on Austria. The anxious Austrians redoubled their efforts to find a peaceful compromise but, when they offered to disarm if the Prussians agreed to do the same, Bismarck glibly remarked that it would be a shame to halt the war preparations when artillery and horses had already been ordered.

Queen Victoria, distraught at what was happening in her beloved Germany, asked Fritz to deliver a letter to his father, suggesting that a congress could settle the dispute. Although he held out little hope of success, Fritz did as she asked, but his father's reply was nothing but a series of complaints about Austria.

'I have not words to express my contempt for the King of Prussia,'[120] the British Foreign Secretary huffed when he read King William's letter, although he told Queen Victoria that he believed that it had been written by Bismarck. He had no doubt, he said, that although the King was 'an honest and honourable man, he has strange delusions about the obligations which honour and honesty impose, but in nothing is his Majesty's power of deluding himself more strongly displayed than in his belief that he is not influenced by his Minister.'[121]

Queen Victoria was so infuriated that she wanted to send British troops to prevent the Prussians from annexing the duchies, but her ministers reminded her that the country had nothing to gain from the conflict, and that, since Britain had remained neutral in the Schleswig-Holstein War 'she cannot interfere in the division of the spoils.'[122]

Chapter 10 – Humble & Modest About All That He Has Done

In his study in the New Palace, Fritz studiously pored over maps of central Europe. As war was now inevitable, he had two overriding aims: to secure a Prussian victory; and to use that victory to bring about German unification.

"One is glad to observe a noticeable change in the views and temper of the Crown Prince," wrote the Minister of War. "He recently told the officers on parade that he had been wrong in opposing Bismarck's policy, for he now saw that the war was unavoidable, etc. He evidently wishes his remarks to be made public."[123]

On 19th May, he was appointed Commander-in-Chief of the Second Army and, the following week, the King named him Military Governor of Prussian Silesia. In early June, he set out to reconnoitre the Silesian terrain and to assure the people that he was there as their protector. From his headquarters in the sixteenth-century Renaissance castle, Schloss Furstenstein, he secured the province's defences by stationing the Silesian army near the fortified town of Neisse.

The local people were touched by his 'quiet kindness' and his concern for their welfare; and, in their letters home, the soldiers under his command praised him so highly that parents of new recruits were often heard to say, 'It's all right if they join the Crown Prince, they will be in good hands.'[124]

Praise, though, did little to assuage Fritz' own insecurities as he doubted his own abilities and feared that he had been promoted too quickly. When he confessed to an elderly General that he felt awkward giving orders to more experienced soldiers, the General assured him that he need not worry as it was his 'duty and part of your calling, as a prince of our royal house, to take high command, and we shall all obey you cheerfully and willingly.'[125]

His anxieties were compounded by news from home, where his two-year-old son, Sigismund, had fallen ill with suspected meningitis. On 19th June, his mother suddenly appeared in Niesse, bearing the tragic tidings that the little boy had died[m]. Heartbroken, he longed to return home to comfort Vicky, whose intense grief was exacerbated by the cruelty of her critics. One malicious article stated that the child's death was a blessing, sent by God to soften the Crown Princesses hard heart. A false rumour spread that she was using the tragedy to persuade Fritz to abandon his troops and return to Berlin. In fact, when Fritz' Chief of Staff paid her a brief visit, she begged him to ensure that on no account her husband should return home.

"I had always believed," the Chief of Staff confessed, "that it was she who kept him away from the front, and was accordingly astonished at finding her the heroine she is.'[126]

Wounded by the slurs, Vicky fled from Berlin to the village of Heringsdorf on the Baltic island of Usedom, to grieve in private with her children. For Fritz, though, there was little time for mourning as, within hours of his mother's visit, his father ordered him to move a section of his troops to the rural district of Landeshut. The next day, he received further news: war had been declared and he must ready himself for battle. His first duty was to issue a proclamation to his troops:

> "Soldiers of the Second Army! You have heard the words of our King and Commander-in-Chief! The attempts of his Majesty to preserve peace to our country have proved fruitless. With a heavy heart, but with strong confidence in the spirit and valour

---

[m] See Chapter 12

of his army, the King has determined to do battle for the honour and independence of Prussia, and for a new organization of Germany on a powerful basis. I, placed by the grace and confidence of my royal father at your head, am proud, as the first servant of our King, to risk with you my blood and property for the most sacred rights of our native country. Soldiers! for the first time for fifty years a worthy foeman is opposed to our army. Confident in your prowess, and in our excellent and proved arms, it behoves us to conquer the same enemy as our greatest King defeated with a small army. And now, forward with the old Prussian battle-cry: 'With God, for King and Fatherland.'"[127]

Although the possibility of defeat still weighed on his mind, Fritz was encouraged by the thought that his father's foresight in increasing military spending had ensured that his men were equipped with the most modern weaponry, including the latest version of the Dreyse needle guns, which fired more shots and were more easily reloaded than the Austrians' muzzle-loading rifles.

Well-armed, well-disciplined and well-led, the Prussian divisions swept through Bohemia achieving victory after victory; and, on a blisteringly hot day in late June, Fritz led his men through some of the most difficult terrain to the Bohemian town of Nachod. They arrived shortly after noon, by which time a battle had been raging for several hours and the Prussians had sustained heavy losses. Fritz ordered a cavalry charge, which put the Austrian cavalry to flight, and turned the tide of the battle.

When news of the victory reached Berlin, bells rang and toasts were raised to the Crown Prince and his fellow commanders, but the greatest cheers were reserved for Bismarck, who, for the first time, was feted as the patriot who would restore Prussian prestige and turn the kingdom into the most formidable force in Central Europe.

In Bohemia, there was no time to indulge in self-congratulations, as a cholera epidemic spread through the region, killing in equal numbers soldiers and civilians. This did not prevent the King from repairing to the general headquarters to take personal command of his armies in what he hoped would be the most decisive moment of the war.

At four o'clock in the morning of 3rd July, Fritz' Chief of Staff woke him with an order from Moltke to set out for the fortress of Koniggrätz[n] to join forces with several other divisions. At first light, he led his men through overgrown woods, steep hills and deep valleys until, at two-thirty in the afternoon, came the echoes of a battle.

From a hill overlooking the scene, the King, Bismarck and Roon had been watching the ebb and flow of the fighting with rising consternation. The Austrians were in the ascendancy and it appeared that they were about to emerge victorious, until, as at Nachod, Fritz appeared and immediately inspired the troops with greater zeal and confidence. He threw himself into the thick of the fighting and 'showed himself perfectly cool and collected, cheerful and bright.' Within an hour, his cavalry broke through the enemy lines.

"A great battle fought near Koniggrätz," the Duke of Cambridge recorded, "between the whole Prussian and Austrian Armies, in which the eight Prussian Corps took part and five Austrian Corps, besides the Saxons…The Needle Musket of the Prussians, it appears, is so offensive that all the gallantry of the Austrians cannot stand up against it. The slaughter seems to have been terrific, and the losses on both sides fearful. The battle lasted eight hours. Prince Frederick Charles[o] first engaged the

---

[n] The Battle of Koniggrätz is also known as the Battle of Sadowa.

enemy with the first Army, but could not make way against her, but in the afternoon the Crown Prince of Prussia came up with the second Army and took the Austrians on flank and rear, which decided the fate of the day.'"[128]

The Austrian commanders sounded the retreat and, as soon as victory was secured, Fritz 'rode among the troops, praising and congratulating them, caring for the wounded, talking with all he could, and encouraging all.'[129]

Overjoyed, the King warmly hugged his son and, removing his own order *Pour Le Merite,* he placed it over his shoulders. Fritz burst into tears as did many of the watching soldiers, who were deeply moved by the unexpected and unfamiliar display of affection. 'Your Majesty,' Moltke told the King, 'has not only won this battle, but also the whole campaign.'

In spite of a few minor skirmishes in the days that followed, the Austrians knew they were beaten and, on 22nd July, they formally sued for peace. The following morning, when the Prussian War Council met, the King and the majority of his Generals agreed to ignore the Austrians' request, and to press onwards so that they could enter Vienna in triumph. Bismarck, however, warned that, if the Austrians were humiliated, they would be filled with such resentment that they would form an alliance with France; and there was a strong possibility that, while the King's armies were marching to Vienna, Napoleon III would seize the Rhineland.[p]

King William, buoyed by success, paid no attention to Bismarck's dull warnings and, although he grudgingly agreed to forego the triumphant march into Vienna, he insisted on continuing the war until Austria was completely humiliated.

---

[o] Prince Frederick Charles was Fritz' cousin – the son of his father's brother, Charles.

[p] See Chapter 13

'My two great difficulties,' Bismarck later declared, 'were first to get King Wilhelm into Bohemia and then to get him out again. Once the King had tasted the sweets of success, he became more difficult to manage.'[130]

When he protested, the King rebuked him and a bitter argument ensued, leaving the exasperated statesman so distraught that he returned his fourth-storey rooms, intending to throw himself out of the window!

At that crucial moment, Fritz appeared in the doorway and quietly told the statesman that he supported his position as the troops were too exhausted to continue.

"You know that I was against this war," he said, placing his hand on Bismarck's shoulder. "You considered it necessary, and the responsibility for it lies on you. If you are now persuaded that our end is attained, and peace must now be concluded, I am ready to support you and defend your opinion with my father."[131]

By the time that Fritz approached him, the King was in a more co-operative mood and, when the details had been set before him, he relented and agreed to begin peace negotiations.

Fritz returned to Berlin on 4th August, but any joy he might have felt in victory was overshadowed by the starkness of the absence of his son. In the midst of the war, his responsibilities had distracted him from his grief, but now the loss struck him more deeply. It had been difficult, he told the Berlin officials, to be separated from his wife as their child was dying, but 'it was a sacrifice which I offered to my country.'[132] A visited to Sigismund's sepulchre brought home to him the enormity of that sacrifice.

"To know that one's child is in the grave," he wrote to a cousin, "is a thought which we mortals cannot realize until we stand before the tomb itself in all its horrible reality. Such experiences rob life of all charm that still remained to it, and only the thought of duty gives one courage to go on living."[133]

He at least had the comfort of being re-united with his other children and with Vicky, who noted that he looked thinner and his new beard made him look older but he was physically well and 'humble and modest about all he has done.'[134]

As Bismarck insisted on treating the Austrians justly during the peace negotiations, Franz Josef was forced only to cede Venetia to Italy[q], and to give an assurance that Austria would play no further part in German affairs. Such leniency was not to be extended to the German states that had fought against Prussia, and, despite their rulers' pleas for more reasonable terms, Fritz agreed with Bismarck that the harshest penalties must be imposed upon them.

> "All the Ministers from South Germany are here," wrote Bismarck's secretary on 10th August. "...Influences are being brought to bear upon the King from various quarters, in favour of the dispossessed Princes, but he remains firm, and is even hard towards the Elector of Hesse. The Crown Prince also stands firm. The campaign and the gravity of the time have done him good, and not the least result is that he has been drawn more to Bismarck, particularly in relation to foreign affairs, and to German policy."[135]

Queen Victoria's cousin, the King of Hanover was sent into exile and his kingdom was annexed by Prussia; Alice's Hesse-Darmstadt was forced to cede a large area of land and given an enormous fine of three million florins, as well as twenty-five thousand florins a day to maintain a Prussian army of occupation. Bavaria was permitted to remain an independent kingdom in exchange for thirty

---

[q] Officially, Venetia was ceded to Napoleon III of France on the understanding that he would immediately cede the province to Italy.

million florins and the abolition of toll charges on the Rhine. Württemberg and Baden were fined eight million and six million florins respectively; and, as well as reparation payments of nine million florins, Saxony was forced to give Prussia a strategic castle; rights to the railway; and the joint occupation of Dresden. Hesse-Kassel, Hesse-Nassau, and Frankfurt were incorporated into Prussia; and Schleswig-Holstein became a Prussian province.

A rumour spread that Vicky had tried to obtain more favourably terms for the King of Hanover but this was far from the truth. When Queen Victoria asked Fritz to intercede on her cousin's behalf, Vicky replied unsympathetically:

> "At this sad time, one must separate one's feelings for one's relations quite from one's judgement of political necessities, or one would be swayed to and from on all sides…they were told beforehand what they would have to expect…as rivers of blood had flowed and the sword decided this contest, the victor must makes his own terms and they must be hard ones for many…We have made enormous sacrifices and the nation expects them not to be in vain. This is the only answer I can give you at present."[136]

No victory would be complete without a triumphal parade, and, from mid-September, craftsmen worked day and night to prepare the streets of Berlin. Flags and bunting bedecked churches, palaces, parks, houses and civic buildings; and captured enemy guns, crowned with wreathes, were set out in rows along the Unter den Linden. A garlanded arch was built around the Brandenburg Gate, topped with flags surrounding the statue of Victory.

At eleven o'clock in the morning of 20th September, the King left his palace on horseback, followed by Fritz and his cousin, Prince Frederick Charles. Behind them a series of carriages carried the Queen and Vicky and her children, in front of rows and rows of marching soldiers from every battalion. Crowds lined the route and crushed into every available window to catch a glimpse of the returning heroes; and, that evening, as the King hosted a dinner for over a thousand officers, a torchlight procession wound its way through the streets of the capital.

Chapter 11 – Sunset From the Mount of Olives

For the duration of the victory parade, Fritz enjoyed a brief moment of glory but, when the cheering faded and the garlands withered, Bismarck had little use for the heir to the throne. From the moment he took up arms, Fritz had viewed the war as a step towards unification, and, when Prussia emerged victorious, he declared that the other German kingdoms should be reduced to dukedoms, regardless of opposition from their people or their sovereigns. When, however, he told Bismarck that his father should immediately be named King of Germany, the statesman casually replied that several states already had their own kings.

Unlike Fritz, who was eager to capitalise on his victories, Bismarck believed in long-term solutions rather than hastily-made plans. Ignoring Fritz' suggestion that the northern states should be subsumed into Prussia, he established instead the North German Confederation: theoretically an alliance of equals, but practically a collection of states under Prussian domination. This was the first major step on the road to unification, as it introduced common tariffs and passports; free movement; and a unified postal system. Most significantly, it led to the formation of a joint parliament: the Reichstag, which was to be presided over by the King of Prussia and his successors.

As Bismarck steadily adhered to his own carefully-prepared schemes, he saw Fritz' suggestions as nothing more than an inconvenient irritation. He had little faith in the Crown Prince's ability to understand the intricacies of his own machinations, and remained convinced that he was too easily influenced by his wife's 'English constitutionalism', which was detrimental to Prussia's progress.

In the aftermath of the Austro-Prussian War, the animosity between Vicky and Bismarck became more apparent. Vicky could not conceal her resentment of the statesman's popularity or her belief that he had claimed Fritz' victories as his own; and, while sitting beside him at dinner, she accused him of serving his own ambition and told him bluntly that she did not trust him.

"She had," Bismarck concluded, "...allowed herself to be influenced in her judgement of my character by further-reaching calumnies. I was ambitious, she said, in a half-jesting tone, to be a king or at least president of a republic. I replied in the same semi-jocular tone that...I had grown up in the royalist traditions of the family and had need of a monarchical institution for my earthly well-being: I thanked God, however, I was not destined to live like a king, constantly on show, but to be until death the king's faithful subject."[137]

Later, he confessed that he pitied but did not respect her because 'a gentlewoman who dabbles in politics herself forgets her gentlewoman's rights.'[138]

Ironically, Vicky was motivated solely by a desire to protect Fritz' position, but her devotion to him and her dislike of Bismarck achieved the opposite result. The greater her antipathy towards him, the deeper became Bismarck's conviction that she opposed his plans because she wanted Prussia to adopt an English constitution; and the happier her marriage, the less Bismarck felt able to trust Fritz with confidential information, for fear he would share it with her, and she would in turn pass it on to her mother in England. Consequently, he excluded Fritz from affairs of state; and to prevent him from 'infecting' his father with the same English ideas, he kept him away from Berlin as often as possible by persuading the King to send him to far-flung locations as his representative.

Within weeks of his return from the war, Fritz was dispatched to Russia for the wedding of the Tsarevich Alexander and Princess Dagmar of Denmark, the sister of the Princess of Wales. As Bertie, the Prince of Wales, had not yet forgiven Fritz for his role in the seizure of Schleswig-Holstein, Queen Victoria feared a frosty meeting in St Petersburg. To avoid a public display of disharmony, she asked Bertie to visit Berlin on his way to Russia, in the hope that he and Fritz could restore their former friendship before the wedding[r]. On arriving in Berlin, Bertie was most put out to discover that Fritz had already left, but the King compensated for his son's apparent snub by attending a dinner party given by Vicky in her brother's honour. This congeniality salved Bertie's hurt feelings, and, when the brothers-in-law met in St Petersburg, past disputes were finally forgotten.

The following year, Fritz and Bertie met again when Napoleon III, keen to show off the vast improvements to his capital, invited princes and statesmen from around the world to the 'Paris Exposition'. The brothers-in-law were seen laughing together as they were driven in the state coach of Louis XVI, which had been recommissioned specifically for the occasion.

His renewed friendship with Fritz meant a great deal to Bertie, particularly at a time when he had become deeply unpopular at home. The public was appalled to read that, while his pregnant wife was seriously ill with rheumatic fever, Bertie stayed at the Windsor Races, ignoring telegrams urging him to return to home. When he eventually returned to London, he continued to entertain his rowdy friends during Alexandra's long recuperation, which created such ill-feeling that he was hissed at the theatre and jeered whenever he appeared in public.

---

[r] The Princess of Wales, who was pregnant, was deemed unfit to make the long journey from England to Russia.

Bismarck relished the scandalous stories about Bertie's promiscuousness as they provided him with another excuse to denigrate Vicky and Britain. On returning to Berlin, he let it be known that the King was disgusted by Bertie's philandering in Paris; and, in the weeks that followed, he spread a series of salacious rumours about his licentiousness and decadent behaviour.

"There is not a horror in Germany that is not told of Bertie," Vicky complained to Queen Victoria, "and how he and Alix [the Princess of Wales] are represented as a wretched couple and you a most unhappy mother. Bertie is supposed to be much disliked in England. This is so much believed in society that it is quite tiresome."[139]

Not content, though, with smearing Vicky and preventing Fritz from participating in affairs of state, Bismarck also sought to separate him from liberal-minded contacts by systematically removing his friends or trusted advisors, including Ernest Stockmar, from office.

"The object of Bismarck has been, and is, to isolate the Crown Prince from all persons not immediately under his (Bismarck's) influence," a British diplomat reported. "He knows that the Prince is a man of unsanguine character, and that this isolation acts upon him in a depressing manner, and he believes that he can depress him into submission."[140]

Bismarck, however, was wrong to believe that Fritz was easily led by others' opinions, or that Vicky always placed British interests above those of Prussia. When disagreements arose between the two countries or the two Royal Families, Fritz invariably demonstrated his allegiance to Prussia, and Vicky invariably stood by her husband. In 1868, for example, Fritz' cousin, Abbat[s], presented himself as a suitor for Vicky's sister, Louise, but

---

[s] Prince Albert of Prussia 1837-1906

as neither Queen Victoria nor Louise favoured the match, the proposal was soundly rejected. Fritz strongly objected to the way that his cousin had been treated; and in a show of solidarity, Vicky refused to deliver a letter from her mother to King William. It would be an affront to the King's dignity, she stated curtly, to receive a communication from a fellow sovereign through a go-between. The dispute intensified when Queen Victoria sanctioned Louise's marriage to the Marquess of Lorne. Fritz was aghast that a princess was permitted to marry 'a commoner', and Vicky complained to her mother that he was upset that she had allowed such a demeaning arrangement[†].

Fritz, meanwhile, continued his travels, which took him to Italy in the spring of 1868, for the wedding of his friend, Prince Umberto – the future King of Italy - and Princess Margherita of Savoy. The following year, he and Vicky's brother-in-law, Prince Louis of Hesse-Darmstadt, toured the Greek islands and the Holy Land on their way to Egypt for the grand opening of the Suez Canal. Bethlehem, Bethany, the Lebanon, the Hebron Valley and Damascus moved him deeply, but nowhere could compare with Jerusalem.

> "I shall never, as long as I live, forget," he wrote in his diary, "that first evening in Jerusalem, when I saw the sunset from the Mount of Olives, and that wondrous peace of Nature supervened which even in any other place has a solemn character of its own. Here the spirit could lift itself over earthly things, and dwell uninterruptedly in those thoughts which move the heart of every Christian when he looks hack on that great work of redemption, which found upon this hallowed spot its loftiest expression. To read over

---

[†] The dispute continued until October 1870 when Louise and Lorne were officially engaged.

again one's favourite passages in the Gospels at such a place is in itself an act of worship."[141]

In mid-November he and Louis arrived at Port Said on the Egyptian coast, where the Khedive was waiting aboard his yacht to welcome six thousand illustrious guests, including the Austrian Emperor; the Prince of Holland; the French Empress Eugenie; and Grand Duke Michael of Russia.

> "It was a gorgeous and a glittering scene at the doorway of the desert, there were fifty men-of-war flying the flags of all nations of Europe, firing salutes, playing their bands, whilst the sandy littoral was covered with tented Arabs and Bedouin from far and near who had come with their families, on horseback and camel to join in the greatest festival that Egypt had seen since the days of the Ptolemies."[142]

The Khedive had arranged magnificent entertainments to celebrate the spectacular opening of the canal; and Louis and Fritz enjoyed firework displays and cruises along the Nile, before departing for Italy, and then on to Cannes, where their wives and children were staying. After spending Christmas in the south of France, Fritz and Vicky left for Paris where they were warmly received by Emperor Napoleon III and Empress Eugenie.

They returned to Prussia in time for the social season, with its endless banquets, receptions and dances. Fritz and Vicky themselves arranged a stunning masked ball, which began with the performance of three consecutive ballets, followed by dancing and dining for the numerous guests, including the King and Queen.

> "A greater success I never saw," one attendee reported. "...The Crown Prince appeared in four different masks, and was full of fun, so much so that the King and Queen, who did not recognise him, at one time proposed that he should be turned out. The King looked well in plain clothes with the ger and a

blue domino; the Crown Princess as Jane Seymour, a beautiful dress, and Prince Henry of Hesse in a dress of the same date, very handsome and becoming."[143]

For all the exotic journeys and the fun of the season, nothing brought Fritz greater contentment than spending time alone with his family. 'The Crown Prince,' observed Catherine Radziwill, 'seemed to me never to have been a happy man except in his family life.'[144] When the season was over and his duties permitted, he withdrew to the New Palace, where he tried to give his children the stability and paternal affection that had so often been denied him.

Chapter 12 – No Parents Could Have Shown More Interest in Their Children

Amid all the rejoicing after William's birth in 1859, no one initially realised the far-reaching consequences of the trauma that the baby had endured. The doctor's use of forceps followed by vigorous shaking had damaged the nerves in William's neck, which led to what would later be known as Erb's palsy[u]. At times, his head jerked uncontrollably; and, as his left arm failed to develop, Vicky noticed that he had difficulty crawling and seemed unaware that his arm even existed. The court doctor, Wenger, experimented by sticking pins in his hands to see if he felt pain, before strapping his right arm to his side in the hope that it would compel him to use the other. The experiment failed, and, as William grew, his disability became more pronounced: he could not keep pace when running with other boys of his age; he could not hold a knife and fork or dress himself; and his balance was affected, making it difficult for him to learn to ride.

Had he not been the eldest child, Fritz and Vicky might have been less concerned, but a future Prussian monarch was expected to be physically perfect, and, even in his early childhood, there were cruel mutterings that 'a one-armed man can never be king.'

"It is a thousand pities he should be so afflicted," Vicky wrote to Queen Victoria, "…it disfigures him so much, gives him something awkward in all his movements, which is sad for a prince…and it is hard that it should be our eldest that has this misfortune."[145]

Distraught that she had failed to produce a perfect heir, Vicky fretted 'night and day' as she desperately tried to find a cure. Various doctors recommended increasingly

---

[u] Erb's palsy is named after the German neurologist, Wilhelm Heinrich Erb (1840-1921)

bizarre and painful treatments, including strapping him into a mechanic device designed to stretch the nerves in his neck; or hanging heavy weights from his arm in the hope that they would make grow. These barbaric and agonising procedures left him too exhausted to attend his lessons, which led his highly-intelligent mother to believe that he was slow-witted and lazy. Hearing her sighs, William mistook her concern for revulsion and came to the erroneous conclusion that he was a disappoint and that she could never love him.

While Vicky wrung her hands in despair and searched for new treatments, Fritz calmly stayed at William's side as he underwent surgery to prevent his head from shaking. When it became clear that there was no cure for his atrophied arm, Fritz decided to abandon the painful treatments and to help him instead to adapt to his disability. Fritz taught him to swim and to row a boat and, despite his frequent falls from his pony, he ordered his tutor to force him to remount until he became a highly skilled horseman. His clothes were designed with raised pockets to hide the shortened limb; and a special utensil – a cross between a knife and a spoon – was devised to enable him to eat without assistance.

Eighteen months after William's birth, a daughter, Charlotte, was born, who also brought little comfort to her mother. Ungainly and thin, her hair was so fine that it had to be cropped like a boy's; and she was such a nail-biter that Vicky strapped her hands to her sides and made her wear gloves all day, in an effort to break the habit. A second son, Henry, was more amenable and amusing, but Vicky frankly told her mother that he was 'ugly.'

The King and Queen, who insisted on playing a major role in the three children's upbringing, praised them constantly and filled them with a sense of their own importance. Queen Victoria was most put out when Charlotte refused to shake hands with her favourite

Highland servant, John Brown, but, when she complained about it, Vicky replied sadly that she was well aware of her children's arrogance but she was powerless to correct them as their faults had 'been hitherto more encouraged than checked.'

Bismarck, too, callously carried his campaign against the English influence into the heart of Fritz' family. He constantly reminded William of his importance as second-in-line to the throne, and filled his head with tales of Prussian glories until Vicky's liberal views seemed weak and 'unPrussian.' Sadly, Vicky's radical honesty exacerbated the situation as she made no secret of her disappointment that her children failed to meet her own high academic standards. When William proudly paraded his first military uniform, she remarked that looked 'like some unfortunate, little monkey dressed up'; Charlotte, was 'so very dull and backward'[146]; and 'poor' eight-year-old Henry, who had 'not grown prettier' [147], 'mortified' her feelings by his resemblance to Fritz' cousin, the reputedly unattractive Princess Marie of the Netherlands[148]. Even Queen Victoria, who never recoiled from describing others' shortcomings, felt a need to protest when Vicky complained that her children were unintelligent. It was not advisable, said the Queen, to press them too hard, as 'more harm than good is done by forcing delicate and backward children.'[149] Although her criticism was sharp, she was equally quick to offer praise: Henry was 'a great darling' whom everyone admired; and William was 'a dear, interesting, charming boy'[150] who, to her surprise, remained cheerful and good-tempered despite his disability.

Sadly, the spies in her household, reported and exaggerated tales of her supposed 'cruelty.'

> "The Crown Princess in the nursery," William's tutor reported, "soon came to be a frequent topic of talk with the Berliners, among whom there even circulated mythical stories of corporal punishment

publicly administered to dirty-faced Princes. The grain of truth at the bottom of these stories was that the mother's love for her children was great, and equal to any effort to bring out everything that was good in them."[151]

Fritz had a far less fraught relationship with his children, for, although his duties often kept him away from home, he had a natural gift for relating to them on their own level. In the evenings when his duties permitted, he loved to sit with his sons, pointing out maps and pictures in history books, and, as they listened enthralled to his accounts of ancient battles, he was quick to warn them not to be deceived by images of glory as, in reality, wars were bloody and cruel. He found a clever means too of correcting their faults, without the need for sharp criticism or reprimands. When, for example, William's nurses complained that their little charge refused to be bathed, Fritz quietly told the sentries not to present arms to him as was the custom. The soldiers obeyed and, when the affronted William balked at their negligence, Fritz calmly explained that they had orders never to salute an unwashed prince.

By the time that the fourth child, Sigismund was born in 1864, Fritz and Vicky had sufficient confidence to insist on taking complete control of his upbringing. For the first time, Vicky defied convention by disregarding the wishes of her mother and her mother-in-law by choosing to breast feed the baby.

Whereas Queen Victoria confessed that she preferred children when they reached five or six years old, Vicky indulged in what her mother referred to as 'baby-worship'. According to Princess Catherine Radziwill, she:

> "...desired with unutterable longing to keep them always in babyhood. She loved them as long as they were quite small with a violence as if she feared they would be taken from her."[152]

Sigismund was a particularly attractive child, who was, wrote Vicky, 'more to me than [his] brothers and sisters...Fritz and I idolised him – he had such dear and winning ways, and was like a little sunbeam in the house.'[153]

It was unfortunate that the fifth child, Moretta[v], was only eight weeks old when Sigismund died, and consequently her earliest experiences were shrouded in excessive mourning. She became desperately shy and had horror of elderly ladies dressed in black, but Vicky, still grieving for Sigismund, found comfort in the 'dear little thing,' who was 'very like her poor little brother – so merry, so good.'[154] Much to Vicky's delight, Moretta always viewed herself as English and, for a while, refused to speak a single word in German. She was undoubtedly Fritz' favourite daughter and, the more he indulged her, the more impetuous she became, prompting Queen Victoria to remark that she had 'been allowed more liberty than I think was prudent.'[155]

When Moretta was eighteen months old, a third son, Waldemar was born – a high-spirited and fun-loving boy, whom Vicky considered 'so much more gifted than his brothers.' Cheerful and charming, he went some way to consoling his parents for the loss of Sigismund; and, like his father, he had 'such an open, fine, manly disposition.'[156]

Two further daughters followed in 1870 and 1872: Sophie – an 'ugly' name in Queen Victoria's opinion – and Margaret, commonly known as Mossy, who was again 'a little sunbeam' despite her mother's gloomy prediction that she would be a charming person one day 'but I fear not a very happy one, for she is so sensitive and her little heart so tender and warm and loving, so clinging that she is sure to suffer in life.'[w][157]

---

[v] Victoria Moretta – sometimes referred to as 'Vicky'.
[w] Vicky's prediction tragically proved correct as two of Mossy's sons were killed during the First World War.

In 1863, the King gave Fritz a country estate, Bornstedt, not far from Potsdam, where the family enjoyed the simple pleasures of bucolic domesticity. Fritz and Vicky immersed themselves in the restoration of a rundown manor house, and revived a farm established by Frederick William IV in 1840. Fritz supervised the land management and organised the accounts; and Vicky took charge of the poultry sheds and dairy cattle:

> "It may, indeed, be doubted," wrote a friend of the family, "whether the Prince and Princess found the farm a very good investment financially, but that was of small importance compared with the spiritual refreshment which they derived from this close periodical contact with the simple, natural gifts of mother earth."[158]

At Bornstedt, Fritz enjoyed spending time with his dogs and horses, indulging his love for animals. On the farm, as well as in Berlin and Potsdam, 'not a day passed...without his visiting the stables to feed with his own hand the horses.'[159] The creatures came to recognise his footsteps and visitors were touched to see how they excitedly shook their heads when they heard him approaching.

Vicky painted, spun, and visited the local families; and Fritz enjoyed walking, swimming and boating with his sons. Children from the local school sometimes came to play with the young princes, one of whom reported that:

> "No parents could have shown more interest in their children than the then Crown Prince and Princess. They were generally present during the simple evening meal which consisted largely of the things I liked best, milk and nursery cake and stewed fruit. They had a smile and kind word for each of their little guests."[160]

Beyond Bornstedt, there were family outings to museums and the Botanical Gardens; holidays at various seaside resorts; and visits to their many relations.

Surprisingly, considering Vicky's own extensive education, neither she nor Fritz placed a great deal of emphasis on their daughters' curriculum beyond ensuring that they acquired the necessary accomplishments of princesses and future wives. Much thought, however, went into the boys' lessons, which included a combination of academic, physical and practical subjects. They were regularly taken to factories to familiarise themselves with industrial processes and working conditions, and, on leaving, they were expected to doff their caps and thank the workers for their time. On the recommendation of the English diplomat, Robert Morier, the somewhat uncouth and 'crotchety' Georg Hinzpeter was appointed as the boys' tutor, despite Ernest Stockmar's warning that he was a 'a hard Spartan idealist.' His critics complained that he been chosen solely because he was an outspoken opponent of Bismarck, and that he intended to ingratiate himself with William because he 'nursed serious hopes of one day ruling over Germany in the name of his pupil.'[161] If that were his true intention, he made little effort to achieve it, as William was unimpressed by his dull and uninspiring lessons:

> "Joyless as the personality of this dry, pedantic man, with his gaunt meagre figure and parchment face, grown up in the shadows of Calvinism, was his educational system; joyless the youth through which I was guided by the 'hard hand' of the Spartan idealist."[162]

Moreover, unbeknown to Fritz, Hinzpeter came to dislike Vicky, and did little to encourage good relations between her and her son. Believing he alone should take charge of the boys' curriculum, he balked at Vicky's 'interference' and remarked in his pupils' that she was too absorbed in her husband to show any real affection to her children.

For all his faults, however, Hinzpeter had the princes' welfare at heart when he suggested that they would benefit from attending a public school to compete with their peers. The idea was so novel that Fritz initially dismissed it out of hand, but, as Hinzpeter persisted, he realised that the company of boys of their own age might prove to be very good for his sons. The King was horrified by the prospect of future monarch sharing a classroom with his future subjects, but this was one issue in which Fritz was prepared to stand up to his father, and boys were enrolled in a gymnasium in Hesse-Kassel.

Chapter 13 – 'Our Fritz'

In the summer of 1865, Emperor Napoleon III was enjoying his annual holiday in Biarritz, when he received an unexpected visit from Bismarck. Without wasting time on niceties, the Chancellor explained that he had come to obtain his assurance of French neutrality in the forthcoming Austro-Prussian War. A victorious Prussia, said Bismarck, could form a powerful alliance with France; but a weakened and defeated Prussia would always be 'looking for allies against its powerful Western neighbour.'[163]

Charming, ambitious and possessing a mind 'as full of schemes as a warren is full of rabbits'[164], Napoleon carefully weighed his options before replying. An Austrian victory, he surmised, would leave Prussia too weak to defend the Rhineland in the event of a French invasion; but, on the other hand, why should he go to the trouble of organising his army, when Bismarck might be prepared to pay for his neutrality by giving him 'certain territories' including Luxembourg? Bismarck hinted that he would be amenable to such an arrangement, and, by the time that he left, Napoleon believed that they had come to a formal agreement.

The Emperor, however, had seriously underestimated Bismarck's lack of scruples; and, when the Austro-Prussian War broke out, he realised he had also failed to appreciate the strength of the Prussian army. Shocked by the speed of the Prussian advance, he was aghast to hear of Fritz' victories:

"The future King a good General, too!" he gasped. "That is the last straw!"[165]

Panicked by the thought of Prussia becoming the most dominant force in Europe, Napoleon's ministers urged him to invade the Rhineland while the Prussians were distracted by the Austrian war. At the crucial time, he hesitated, partly because he was afflicted by an agonising abdominal complaint which left him incapable of leading his army, and partly because he believed that if he continued to maintain neutrality, Bismarck would honour their agreement.

In fact, Bismarck was astonished by Napoleon's failure to launch an invasion, and, years later, he told a French diplomat:

> "I don't understand yet why the French army did not cross the Rhine in July, 1866, while we were entangled in the passes of Bohemia. And when I say 'the French army,' I'm wrong: one single division, fifteen thousand men, would have sufficed! The mere sight of your red trousers in the Duchy of Baden and the Palatinate would have raised the whole of Southern Germany against Prussia…And that would have been the end of us. I do not know if we could even have covered Berlin."[166]

When the Austro-Prussian War concluded, Napoleon eagerly anticipated his reward, and was horrified when his scouts report that a Prussian garrison had been established in Luxembourg. He sent emissaries to Bismarck, asking him to withdraw the troops so that France could annex the territory, but Bismarck insultingly laughed that they were 'begging for a tip', before denying that he had ever made such an agreement.

Already affronted, Napoleon was appalled when he learned of the establishment of the North German Confederation, which he viewed as a precursor to a unified Germany. Alarmed by the prospect of a powerful neighbour, he asked Bismarck for a promise of compensation in the event of German unification, and, when he received no reply, he moved his troops to defensive positions along the border.

Fritz, who knew nothing of the Biarritz agreement, saw Napoleon's military manoeuvring as an aggressive the Weissenburg gate, came the soldiers who had been that day engaged in this unequal struggle. They arrived weary, dead beat, having tasted no food for twenty-four hours, mourning a commander, a comrade. They all told the same tale – that it was impossible to keep up the fight; had they only been twenty thousand, they would have driven the enemy back."[177]

Many French soldiers raced towards other garrisons and, in normal circumstances, Fritz would have ordered his troops to give chase, but, due to the speed of his advance, his cavalry divisions had not yet arrived and so the fleeing French were free to fight another day.

Fritz had neither the time nor the inclination to celebrate the victory, as, early the following morning, he led his men on towards the Alsatian village of Worth. As the competent French General MacMahon had amassed a force of over eight-thousand men, Fritz intended to await his cavalry before launching an attack on the 7th August. In the early hours of the 6th, however, he heard the booming of cannon and realised that a battle was underway. At eleven o'clock he reached the battlefield and, for the next six hours, he remained in the saddle in the heart of the fray. Heavy losses were sustained on both sides and, for a while, it appeared that MacMahon would emerge triumphant, but in the late afternoon, the French were forced to retreat, leaving thirty cannon and forty-thousand prisoners in the hands of the triumphant Germans.

Bismarck pointedly failed to acknowledge Fritz' role in the victory, and looked 'as sulky as a bear' when the King warmly praised him; but, with two victories in four days, the morale of the Third Army soared, and 'Our Fritz' became the soldiers' 'idol.'

> "Troops commanded by him in person became practically invincible," wrote one contemporary, "for every soldier in the ranks was stirred by the

provocation; and he was pleased when it prompted the liberals in the Landtag to increase the military budget. He was aghast when his mother insisted that peace must be maintained at all costs, as he agreed with Vicky that, if French posturing continued unchecked, Prussia would lose prestige through 'a semblance of timidity and undue weakness, the fault which for years had so cruelly damaged our interests'[167].

As mistrust and indignation mounted on both sides, war seemed inevitable until January 1870, when a former republican, Emile Ollivier, was elected as the French Prime Minister. Determined to maintain peace, Ollivier ignored Napoleon's warnings of Prussia's belligerence, and introduced a scheme to reduce the size of the French army in a show of his pacific intentions.

Bismarck, though, was keen to provoke the French into a war, which would not only unite the German states against a common enemy but would also sure-up German defences. He involved himself, therefore, in the vexing question of the Spanish succession, which was certain to arouse French indignation. Four years earlier, Queen Isabella had been ousted from the Spanish throne and various candidates had been suggested as her replacement. When several other suggestions had been rejected, Bismarck recommended Prince Leopold of Hohenzollern-Sigmaringen, knowing that the French would object to a kinsman of King William.

> "The Hohenzollerns," wrote the author, Victor Hugo, "have reached such audacity that they aspire to dominate Europe. It will be for our time an eternal humiliation that this project has been, we will not say undertaken, but only conceived."[168]

Napoleon was equally piqued, telling the Prussian ambassador that Prince Leopold's candidacy was 'aimed at France and the country will surely resent it.' Nonetheless, as he did not want war, he told his own ambassador to 'return to Berlin, talk the matter over with Bismarck, but be careful to use no expressions which might lead him to think that we are seeking a quarrel.'[169]

For a while, it appeared that Bismarck was prepared to let the matter drop but, behind the scenes, he began secret negotiations with the leader of the Spanish Provisional Government, General Prim, and he privately assured King William that Leopold was the choice of the Spanish people.

On the morning of 2nd July 1870, Napoleon opened a newspaper and was astounded to read that Leopold had been chosen as the King of Spain. He urgently sent his Foreign Minister, Benedetti, to the Spa town of Ems, where King William was taking the waters, to ask him to reconsider Leopold's position. Much to Bismarck's annoyance, the King insisted on meeting Benedetti alone, and, in the absence of the Machiavellian statesman, their discussion was most cordial. The King agreed that Leopold should renounce any claim to the throne, and he promised to write to the prince's father to ensure that outcome. Delighted, Benedetti asked the King for an assurance that no other Hohenzollern candidate would ever be nominated; and, although the King replied that he could not make such a promise, the meeting concluded amicably.

Not to be deterred, Bismarck asked permission to send the details of the conversation to the press and foreign governments. The King innocently gave his consent, at which Bismarck doctored the transcript to give the impression that Benedetti had been insulted and humiliated.

> "The French Ambassador," he wrote, "having insisted on guarantees for the future, after Prince Leopold's desistance, His Majesty refused to receive him anymore, and sent word to him, by the aide-de-camp on duty, that he had nothing further to communicate to him."[170]

At the same time, he sent a series of anonymous articles to the press, accusing the French Empress of having stirred the Spanish into revolution so that her husband could appoint Queen Isabella's successor. As he had intended, the French were so outraged by the insult that, under pressure from his ministers, Napoleon ordered his army to prepare for war.

News of the French mobilisation spread rapidly through Germany, provoking such patriotism that the states which had been enemies only four years earlier were united in their determination to defeat the French aggressors.

> "...The provocation of a war such as this is a crime that will have to be answered for, and for which there is no justification," wrote Vicky's sister, Alice. "...There is a feeling of unity and standing by each other, forgetting all party quarrels, which makes one proud of the name of German."[171]

On 14th July, Vicky gave birth to her third daughter, Sophie, and five days later Napoleon III issued a declaration of war. Fritz was immediately given command of the German Third Army – a position that was both flattering and daunting. The one-hundred-and-twenty-eight battalions under his command were drawn from several states; and Moltke, the Chief of Staff, explained that he had chosen Fritz as the only man who could inspire loyalty even in those who were known to despise Prussia. 'Moltke felt,' wrote one contemporary observer, 'that it was the Crown Prince alone who could succeed in infusing them with enough patriotism to fight and with sufficient enthusiasm to vanquish the enemy.'[172]

Sophie's christening on 25th July was a sombre occasion as the majority of the male guests were in uniform in preparation for active service. The ceremony was 'sad and serious,' Vicky told her mother; 'anxious faces and tearful eyes, and a gloom and foreshadowing of all the misery in store spread a cloud over the ceremony, which should have been one of gladness and thanksgiving.'[173] When Fritz entered the room, one guest thought that, although he had 'that air of dignity which distinguishes him on State occasions...there was a touch of sadness in his face and voice, mingling with kindliness of manner peculiarly his own.'[174]

The King was so anxious that he could not even hold the baby; and the room was so hot that Vicky had to retire early. Fritz, wondering how many of the uniformed men would return safely to their families, could only steady his nerves by telling himself repeatedly, 'we shall conquer.'

The following day, the family quietly attended a service at Sigismund's mausoleum; and early the next morning before Vicky was awake, Fritz slipped away to join his regiment. Keen to repay that trust that Moltke had placed in him, he did not underestimate the challenges that lay ahead and the real possibility that the Germans would be defeated. The troops of the southern states were neither as well-trained nor as well-disciplined as the Prussians had been in the Austrian war; and the new French chassepot rifles were reputed to be far more effective than the Prussian Dreyse needle guns.

Moltke had urged him to go at once to his new headquarters, but instead he followed Bismarck's advice that he should first visit Bavaria, Württemberg and Baden to meet the troops placed under his command. He set out for Munich and was greeted by the Bavarian King Ludwig II, who, at the age of only twenty-five, had already acquired a reputation for eccentricity. Known for his adulation of Wagner and his construction of fairy-tale castles, Fritz found him 'strangely altered: much less handsome, lost his front teeth, pale, nervous in his speech, does not wait for an answer after putting questions, but while the answer is being given puts other questions referring to widely different subjects.'[175] Nonetheless, although his troops looked 'sluggish', Fritz was happily surprised by their enthusiasm, as one soldier told him that they all believed that, had he been their commander in the Austro-Prussian War, the Bavarians would have 'smashed' the Prussians.

In spite of his eccentricities, King Ludwig was astute enough to recognise that danger that unification posed to his kingdom. Before agreeing to send his troops to war, he had written to Fritz to seek an assurance that, no matter what happened, Bavaria would retain independence. Now, before he left Munich, the King reiterated that he was lending Fritz his men solely on the understanding that his kingdom would remain intact and autonomous.

In Württemberg, Fritz again received an enthusiastic welcome; and flowers were thrown in to his path when he entered Baden. Reassured by the willingness of the troops to accept him as their commander, he came to the conclusion that this sense of shared purpose was a major step on the road to unification.

"It fills me with pride and joy," he said in his first address to his army, "to march against the enemy at the head of the united sons of every part of the German Fatherland, to fight for the common national cause, for German right, for German honour...Let us then stand together like true brothers in arms, and with God's help let us unfurl our standards to new victories, to the glory and peace of our now united Germany."[176]

As reassuring as the support of his men was the realisation that the French troops might not be as effective as he had been led to believe. Many of them looked puny and unfit for battle, and, as they set out from Paris, some were so drunk that they marched out of step with women hanging on their arms.

Fritz' initial objective was to lead his men across the Bavarian border into the thickly-wooded territory of Alsace to secure the German defences and create a gateway to Paris. Anticipating this move, Napoleon had sent reinforcements to bolster the region's garrison towns, one of which, Weissenburg, was placed under the command of a renowned General Abel Douay. On the night of 3rd- 4th August, Fritz sent his artillery onto the Bavarian heights above Weissenburg, while his infantry, camouflaged by the dense foliage, slowly edged closer to the fortifications. At eight o'clock in the morning while the French were still at breakfast, he gave orders for the artillery to open fire. Eventually, when the shelling ceased, the French were horrified to see hundreds of infantrymen rapidly moving towards them across the river. Their first response was to prepared a defensive bayonet charge but they suddenly realised that they were surrounded.

The surprise attack gave Fritz' army a clear advantage, but the French chassepot rifles proved as effective as he had feared. With a longer range and greater accuracy than the Prussian needle-guns, they mowed down the attackers, killing over one hundred German officers in the process. Nonetheless, Fritz' troops pressed on and, by noon, General Douay realised that he had lost the battle. He shot his own horse and, raising his sword, stood directly in the line of fire until he was stuck by a shell and killed instantly. His death left his troops so demoralised that many fled through neighbouring vineyards, and, at two o'clock in the afternoon, the townspeople surrendered.

By the time that Fritz entered Weissenburg, over three-thousand Frenchmen lay dead and most of the survivors had fled. To Fritz' disgust, even the doctors had abandoned their wounded patients, but, in the midst of the chaos and slaughter, General Douay's little dog faithfully stood guarding the body of his late master.

The refugees from Weissenburg flocked into the neighbouring towns, as a French correspondent reported:

"The streets were thronged with people talking over the sad events of the day…Then, pouring through sight of his princely leader to deeds of courage and daring. Even the greatest coward became a hero when he felt the kindly eye of 'Frederick the Noble' upon him. And the eye was indeed a kindly one, in perfect keeping with his gentle demeanour; his unaffected good-nature, his utter absence of self-sufficiency."[178]

He repaid their trust by showing every confidence in his officers, allotting them specific tasks without interfering in the details. The more he entrusted to them, 'the more certain was he that everyone endeavoured to please him, and to act in accordance with his intentions."[179]

He made a point, too, of showing his appreciation of the lower ranks by sharing their hardships and pausing during inspections to shake their hands and address individual soldiers by name. One English journalist, hearing the hearty cheers that greeted his appearance, noted that:

> "The Crown Prince is not indifferent to the easy arts by which Royalty can secure popularity; or, rather, it comes to him naturally, out of his exceeding amiability, to show consideration for others. He knows well how these soldiers like to see their General and their Prince in the flesh, and also how it strengthens an officer's position with his men when Prince and General pay him attention. So we had a great deal of inspections to do, for the Prince rode up, not merely to every battalion, but almost to each company, speaking to the officers in command; and, when he came to the Brigadier, remaining for a few minutes chatting with him and with the members of his Staff."[180]

The British Military Commissioner, who had been assigned to accompany his army, was also impressed by his kindness, good judgement and 'fine and manly character'. The Englishman noticed, too, how chivalrously he behaved towards the enemy, allowing captured French officers to retain their swords and addressing his prisoners respectfully. He visited the wounded Frenchmen to ensure that had all they needed and, on hearing that one captured officer had carried a wounded General from the battlefield, he commended his courage and ordered his release in recognition of his gallantry. When another cuirassier sighed that he was ashamed at having been captured when his comrades had lost everything, Fritz replied, 'You are wrong in saying that you have lost everything, for after you have fought like brave soldiers you have not lost your honour.'[181]

Victory, however, did not lessen his abhorrence of war. Sickened by the bloodshed, he remarked shortly after the Battle of Worth:

> "I detest this butchery. I have never longed for war laurels, and would willingly have left such fame to others without envying them. Yet it is just my fate to be led from one war to another, and from battlefield to battlefield, before I ascend the throne of my ancestors. It is a hard lot."[182]

It was a sentiment he repeated when, in 1871, he fell into conversation with an English Privy Councillor.

> "I like the Crown Prince…the more, the more I see of [him]," wrote the Privy Councillor, Arthur Helps. "He sympathises greatly with me, or rather I with him, in an intense horror of the miseries and cruelties of war."[183]

In the midst of battle, he was often in as much danger as his men and he was no more immune than they were to the diseases that plagued armies in wartime. Towards the end of August, he was struck with a gastro-intestinal infection and for several days he was put on a diet of frumenty[x]. Although he was unfit to ride, he refused to

---

[x] Frumenty – a thick porridge-like broth.

relinquish his duties but arranged to travel between strategic points in a closed carriage.

News from home added to his discomfort, as Vicky had once again become the subject of malicious gossip. Although Britain remained neutral, the French purchased British horses and ammunition, leading Vicky's critics to the unfounded conclusion that she and her sister, Alice, were working for the enemy. Vicky complained to Queen Victoria that Prussia had turned to England for help but 'the first positive indication of England's feelings was the unfortunate sale of coals, ammunition and cartridges!'[184] Nonetheless, suspicions ran so high that the Berliners were reluctant even to allow her to use her considerable talents to organise hospitals for the wounded.

Moltke, meanwhile, had been carefully monitoring Napoleon's movements, and, in late August, he received intelligence that he and General MacMahon were planning to relieve the besieged city of Metz. Moltke sent orders to intercept the Emperor before he reached the city, and, when Napoleon's scouts warned him of an enemy force approaching, he ordered an immediate retreat to the town of Sedan.

'Now we have them in a mousetrap!' Moltke cried exultantly, knowing that the combined German armies of almost a quarter of a million men, could surround the town and decimate Napoleon's force of one-hundred-and-forty-thousand.

Fritz rose before dawn on 1st September, and, shortly after four o'clock, he ascended a hill overlooking Sedan. The town was completely encircled by German troops, and it was clear that Napoleon had been outplayed and outnumbered. When a messenger told him that the French Emperor had slept near Sedan that night, Fritz replied, 'In that case he cannot be very far away, and must know this day is going badly for him;' with 'almost a touch of pity in his tone.'[185]

At six o'clock, the German artillery bombardment began and, for several hours, Sedan was under attack from all directions. The encircling infantry and cavalry surged forwards, and MacMahon was struck in the back by a shell that left him severely wounded. Napoleon, in intense pain, and looking so ill and gaunt that he had taken to wearing make-up, bravely rode out through the thick of the fighting, and drove back a German attack but was unable to retain the advantage. Fritz set a battery of guns to the rear of the French line, to which the French responded with a sustained musket attack which led to many German losses before the musketeers were forced to withdraw.

By late afternoon, the French had sustained seventeen-thousand casualties and a further twenty-one-thousand men had been taken prisoner; and, among over one thousand German fatalities, was the son of the Minister of War, Albrecht von Roon.

Seeing the extent of the slaughter, King William, who was watching from a hilltop, sent a message demanding an immediate surrender but he received no reply and the bombardment continued until most of the town was ablaze. When a rumour spread through the French ranks that revolution had broken out in Paris, dozens of soldiers threw down their arms and deserted or surrendered.

"The fall of the poor Emperor seems imminent," wrote the Duke of Cambridge. "I am so glad, though, that this good fortune should have fallen to the lot of the Crown Prince, a high-minded and generous man and a good soldier in every sense of the word."[186]

At last, a white flag was seen fluttering above the burning town, and King William sent an officer, Colonel von Bonsart, to demand an unconditional surrender. To his astonishment, Bronsart found himself face-to-face with Napoleon, who asked him to take a letter to the King, conceding defeat and stating that, as he had not been killed in action, it was his duty to hand over his sword to the victors.

When Bismarck heard that Napoleon was asking to meet him, he invited him to the nearby town of Donchery where he was staying. Horses were readied and the ailing Emperor set out with one of his Generals and Bronsart but he was so ill he could hardly remain in the saddle.

> "The journey from Sedan was a fearful ordeal for the Emperor," his General recorded. "He could scarcely keep on his horse, he was suffering such pain. He succeeded in doing so, however, by leaning with both hands on the pommel of the saddle, never allowing a single complaint to escape from him."[187]

Approaching Donchery, Napoleon's heart sank at the prospect of encountering bands of French mutineers. Out of pity, Bronsart sent a message to Bismarck explaining the situation, and Bismarck agreed to meet him at a farmhouse outside the town. Face to face on a bench outside the farmhouse, Napoleon acknowledged that he was defeated, and agreed to surrender himself and his army but stated that, as a prisoner, he lacked the authority to negotiate peace. He assumed that his capture would bring an end to the war as he could see no reason why the Germans would want to continue fighting, as he later explained:

> "In a manifesto which the Crown Prince of Prussia published at the moment when he took command of his troops, he said that Germany had taken up arms not against France but against me. So I naturally concluded that if I handed my person over to the King, this would put an end to the conflict and a speedy and satisfactory peace could be brought about."[188]

Seeing how ill he looked, Bismarck did not press him further but arranged for him to be taken to the Chateau de Bellevue, about five miles from Sedan. When he had been given time to rest, King William visited him and, with no show of triumphalism, addressed him with respect and kindness. As the meeting concluded, Fritz arrived and was shocked to see how frail and jaded Napoleon had become.

> "The King's lofty and august figure contrasted admirably with the diminutive and depressed form of the Emperor. When Napoleon caught sight of me, he gave me his hand, while with the other he dried up the big tears trickling down his cheeks. He referred with much gratitude to the language and generous manner generally with which the King had received him. I spoke, of course, in the same spirit, and asked whether he had obtained any night's rest, to which he replied that anxiety about his family had left him no sleep. On my regretting that the war had assumed so frightfully bloody a character, he replied that that was unhappily only too true, and it was all the more frightful *'quand on n'a pas voulu la guerre.'"*[189]

Napoleon was mistaken to assume that his surrender meant an end to the war. As the revolution in Paris had led to the collapse of the government, there was no one with the authority to negotiate terms. Bismarck, therefore, sent an address to the French nation, demanding the cities Strasbourg and Metz and the province of Alsace as the price of peace. In the meantime, Fritz was ordered to continue his march towards Paris, and, when Napoleon learned of his movements, he was disgusted. He had believed Fritz' manifesto but now it appeared that it had been nothing but a ploy devised by Bismarck, 'whose aim was to sow the seeds of discord among Frenchmen and to bring about a fresh trial of the famous system of 'war through internal revolutions.'[190]

Chapter 14 – The Siege of Paris

Riding at the head of his army through the late summer sunshine, Fritz was astounded by the lack of resistance as he moved towards Paris. Only five days after the Battle of Sedan, he had reached the outskirts of Rheims, less than ninety miles from the capital. Approaching the city, he ordered his troops not to requisition the property of the poor, nor to expect to be housed and fed by those who could ill afford it. The locals were so impressed by his concern for their welfare that, when the soldiers entered Rheims, they met no ill-will but were treated with civility.

In the absence of hostility, Fritz enjoyed a few days' rest, wandering freely among the people and visiting the historic sites, including the thirteenth-century Cathedral of Notre Dame, where traditionally the Kings of France had been crowned. He had time, too, to contemplate the devastating effects of a war that had created many widows and orphans, and left many of the wounded unable to find work to support their families. In an effort to alleviate their sufferings, he established a relief fund, and wrote to the heads of all the German states to solicit contributions.

> "As this war," he wrote, "has called out a united German Army, in which the sons of every race are contending in brotherly rivalry for the palm of valour, so let the provision for the invalided and the destitute whom war will leave on our hands be an undertaking which the whole German race shall co-operate in."[191]

Meanwhile in Paris, three prominent republicans formed a provisional Government of National Defence: Louis Trochu, a military commander, who had played a prominent role in the Crimean War; Léon Gambetta, a politician and lifelong republican; and Jules Favre, a statesman who had been among the first to demand the abdication of Napoleon III. As the new Foreign Minister,

Favre took responsibility for the peace negotiations and, in his opening statement, he declared that he was willing to pay reparations and cede overseas territories to the victors but he would not yield a single inch of French soil.

Still revelling in the victory at Sedan, the Prussian commanders were not prepared to accept so paltry an offer; and they sent orders to Fritz to continue towards Paris. On 15th September, he reached the outskirts, and, three days later, the King and Bismarck took up residence in Versailles. As the combined German forces encircled the capital, Fritz went to Versailles pay his respects to his father. On entering the Avenue de Paris, he was met by a silent crowd of stony-faced Frenchmen among whom was one English woman frantically waving a Union Jack in his honour. As soon as he passed through the palace gates, the atmosphere changed dramatically, as a band played and the cheer from the troops was deafening. A correspondent for *The Times* reported:

> "Soldiers ran from all sides to see the Prince, who rode along the ranks of the regiment, and then turned into the court of the Prefecture, after which the guard of honour trooped its colours inside, and the Staff rode off to find their quarters."[192]

For several weeks, the British Government had been trying to mediate between the warring factions, and, on the day that the King arrived in Versailles, a British diplomat persuaded Favre to negotiate directly with Bismarck.

Like Napoleon, Favre had read and believed Fritz' manifesto, which convinced him that Prussians' sole objective was the overthrow of the Emperor. He was horrified when Bismarck issued him with a list of demands, adding, 'Strasburg is the key to our house and we must have it.' He insisted on taking control of Alsace, as the region formed a vital buffer between France and Germany, and, as he later told the Reichstag, it would serve as 'a rampart against the incursions which a passionate and warlike people have been making into our country for two hundred years.'[193]

Favre was so shaken by the enormity of the demands that his eyes filled with tears, and, when he managed to speak, he could only gasp that such terms would dishonour his country. Unmoved, Bismarck coldly replied that, if he failed to comply, the war would continue and, when victory was secured, the Germans would expect far greater recompense for their trouble. Distraught but unyielding, Favre left the meeting, asking only that Bismarck would do him the kindness of not revealing that he had seen him weep.

The next day, Paris was officially placed under siege; and Bismarck, eager to bring the war to an end, urged the King to order an immediate bombardment. Fritz pointed out the logistical difficulties that this would entail, as it required the transport of huge siege guns and vast amounts of ammunition from Prussia. Moreover, he agreed with the King and the General Staff that a bombardment would kill many innocent civilians, which would severely damage the Germans' reputation. Instead, he recommended starving the Parisians into submission, convinced that within a couple of weeks the city would surrender. He did not believe, though, that the fall of Paris would bring an immediate end to the 'horrid' war, as the enemy would continue fighting with increasing bitterness.

> "I only desire durable and honourable peace," he concluded. "We are not ambitious. We do not seek glory as others do. But the war was forced on us; we must exact conditions which will prevent France, out of mere light-heartedness and wantonness, attacking the German nation again."[194]

While the Germans deliberated, the French, anticipating a bombardment, took hasty precautions to protect Paris' treasures, storing works of art in underground bunkers, and placing sandbags against the windows of historic buildings. As they did not expect the Germans to starve them into submission, they saw no need to store adequate provisions for a lengthy siege, particularly when they believed that the city's stocks of animals would provide sufficient food for at least two months.

The French authorities were badly mistaken. By mid-October, supplies were dwindling so rapidly that they were forced to ration meat; and, when all the cattle and sheep had been slaughtered, they were reduced to eating dogs, cats and horses. Even rats were seen as a delicacy and, at Christmas, zoo animals appeared on menus, including the star attractions, Castor and Pollux, two elephants that were sold to a restaurant for twenty-seven-thousand francs.

Numerous unsuccessful attempts were made to break the siege, and small bands of guerrillas regularly launched sorties against the Germans. More imaginative Parisians ascended in hot air balloons to scatter republican leaflets onto the German lines, urging them to follow the French example by overthrowing their king so that they could return home to their families. Fearing that the messages could undermine the troops' morale, the Germans invented a rotating gun to shoot the balloons from the sky, but the balloonists took to flying under cover of darkness, which enabled them to deliver mail to the surrounding towns.

As the Parisians' only means of obtaining news was by pigeon post, which was notoriously unreliable, rumours were rife about what was happening outside the city. Some claimed that Fritz, Molke and Bismarck wanted to negotiate but they were prevented from doing so by King William, whom, for some reason, the Parisians nicknamed 'the mystic drunkard.' Others blamed Fritz for deceiving them with his false manifesto, and warned that if he appeared on the streets, he would be instantly assassinated. The press reported that Moltke was dead, Fritz was dying of a fever, and Bismarck was terrified of the obstinate King William.

As ever, there was also gossip in Prussia, where the public, impatient for an end to the war, could not understand why the King had not ordered a bombardment. Fritz sighed that Bismarck's daughter, 'points me out to all and sundry as more particularly the guilty cause of its postponement,' but he was more dismayed by the gossips' assertion that he was acting under Vicky's influence.

"In Berlin," he noted bitterly, "it is the order of the day to vilify my wife as being mainly responsible for the postponement of the bombardment of Paris and to accuse her of acting under the direction of the Queen of England...But who in Berlin can judge what is best to do before Paris? Did we by any chance consult these wiseacres about Weissenburg, Worth, and Sedan? I should like these experts to come along here...and show whether they understand the job better than we do!"[195]

Since the middle of August, Metz and Strasbourg had also been besieged but, on 28th September, under a sustained bombardment Strasbourg surrendered. A month later, starvation forced Metz to follow suit, and King William was so delighted that he promoted Fritz and his cousin, Prince Frederick Charles, to the rank of Field Marshal.

Beyond the siege, life continued relatively peacefully for the French citizens, who went about their business as though the country were not at war. From his headquarters in Versailles, Fritz assured the local people that he would act as their protector and, within hours of his arrival, he proved that he would be true to his word. A Dutch doctor, Mr Vandervelde, who had been in charge of a number of hospital trains, told him that the German troops had requisitioned the hospitals, turning out all the French patients regardless of their condition. Fritz instantly sent orders that they must all return to the hospital and beds would be provided for them so that their treatment could continue. The owner of the house in which he stayed was equally impressed by his kindness, writing soon after the war that:

> "Those were indeed bad times, but we thought ourselves happy to be under the protection of that stately and friendly gentleman, who appears to us, as we now think of him, to have been a good genius who warded off mischief from our household. Although, according to the laws of war, he was our master, and the owner for the time of all that we had, he behaved himself always as if he were our guest. I can never forget the gentleness with which he used to ask for anything, whether for himself or his Adjutant, apologising for giving us trouble, fearful of causing any inconvenience, and enquiring whether this or that would interfere with our own arrangements."[196]

In Louis XVI's palace, Fritz established more hospital wards, which he regularly visited to talk with the wounded and to ensure that everything was running smoothly. He took time, too, to visit the French patients, 'with his pocket full of cigars, which he distributed amongst them.'[197]

His diligence contrasted sharply with the decadence of some German princes, including Vicky's uncle, Duke Ernest II of Saxe-Coburg and Gotha[y]. The Duke established his headquarters in a former casino in Versailles from where he indulged his passion for amorous pursuits, expecting the Prussian government to fund his dissolute lifestyle. His behaviour, like that of several other princes, so appalled the Prussians that, when King William heard how they were living, 'some were sent back to the rear or

---

[y] The brother of Prince Albert.

on to the front, the King [of Prussia] wisely thinking them more ornamental than useful in Versailles.'

At Christmas, Fritz received a trunk of gifts from home, including a cake that Vicky had made, which he shared with the owner of the house in which he was staying, but, in spite of the temporary ease and the respite from fighting, he confessed to Queen Victoria that he missed his family so much that he 'felt more inclined often to shed tears than to enjoy a festival time.'[198]

The King, too, was growing weary of the prolonged campaign and, at New Year, he ordered the heavy siege guns to be brought from Prussia in order to launch a bombardment. When the shelling began on 5th January, the horrendous boom of the guns was terrifying but its actual impact was minimal. Children ran through the streets collecting pieces of shell to sell as souvenirs, and a rumour spread that the noise was only a ruse to hide the sound of a German retreat.

Abroad, though, as Fritz had predicted, there was almost universal condemnation of the bombardment, and the British press greatly exaggerated the extent of the damage and the number of casualties. The criticism, Vicky told her mother, sprang not from concern for the Parisians but rather from the fact that the British enjoyed visiting Paris and could not bear the thought of the destruction of their favourite holiday destination. Princess Clementine, a daughter of the deposed King Louis Philippe, wrote an angry letter to Queen Victoria, asking why powerful England failed to halt such barbarism. Although the Queen dismissed the princess' demands as 'insane', she wrote to Fritz' father to tell him of the strength of anti-German feeling.

The King, put out by her interference, replied that the French republican leaders were dictators who refused all reasonable negotiations, before hinting that the Germans had been disappointed by Britain's 'benevolent neutrality', which appeared to favour the French. 'It is certainly most unjust that…I am blamed for the long duration of the war,' he complained before expressing his regret at the disagreement.

> "The anti-German meetings which are on the increase in England are a display which can only augment the irritation of the German people; who…were not prepared for such demonstrations on the part of England."[199]

For three weeks, over a thousand shells rained down on the outskirts of Paris, killing one hundred people, whereas, in the first week of January alone, three-thousand-five-hundred had died of starvation or diseases caused by malnutrition. The bombardment exacerbated the problem of the food supply, as those who lived in the outskirts moved further into the city, disrupting the system of rationing. Meat was no longer available and, by mid-January, bread was not only in short supply but also of a poor quality.

> "Only one kind is allowed to be manufactured;" wrote one resident, "it is dark in colour, heavy, pasty, and gritty. There is as little corn in it as there is malt in London beer when barley is dear. The misery among the poorer classes is every day on the increase."[200]

In a desperate effort to maintain morale, the French press asserted that fifty-thousand Germans had been captured, and Fritz' cousin, Prince Frederick Charles, had been fatally wounded. Optimistic headlines, though, could not feed starving people and, on 19th January, under pressure from the citizens of Paris, Trochu took charge of a final attempt to break through the German lines.

Several French commanders were ordered to move their divisions through the parkland of the Chateau Buzenval, to the west of Paris, towards King William's headquarters at Versailles. In the early morning, concealed by thick fog, the artillery broke through two Prussian barricades and, under Trochu's command, seized the town of Saint Cloud only six miles from Versailles. Despite fierce Prussian resistance, Trochu held the town throughout the day but the other commanders were gradually forced to retreat back to the city.

By nightfall, it was clear that Trochu was isolated, and Fritz, who had been monitoring the French advance, seized the opportunity to retake Saint Cloud. The fighting was intense and at one point a French shell exploded immediately in front of Fritz, but, while his panicking officers urgently asked him to move to safety, he calmly stepped aside in 'a very leisurely manner.'

By two o'clock in the morning, Trochu had retreated, and Saint Cloud had been razed to the ground, leading one witness to compare the devastation to the destruction of Pompeii. Thirty-nine German officers and over six hundred men had been killed; but the French had suffered over three-thousand losses.

French morale sank to the depths and, as the bombardment continued and starvation spread, Favre realised that all was lost and, nine days later, Paris surrendered. Food was hastily shipped into the city, and the new leader of the French Government, Adolphe Thiers, entered into negotiations with Bismarck.

As Bismarck had warned before the siege, the German demands would be severe, including the province of Alsace and a payment of eight million francs in reparations. When Thiers protested that the price was too high, Bismarck agreed to reduce the amount by three million francs in return for the province of Lorraine and the fortified city of Metz. Thiers desperately turned to Fritz, pleading with him to reduce the demands, but he replied that, while he sympathised with Thiers' plight, he fully supported Bismarck.

Finally, on 15th February, Thiers accepted all the demands and signed the peace agreement. 'The joy of our army around Paris is not to be described,' Vicky wrote to Queen Victoria; and, less than a fortnight later, Fritz proudly rode into the city at the head of thirty-thousand Germans. In the days that followed, large sections of the army returned to their families, and when Fritz arrived in Berlin on 17th March, rapturous crowds welcomed home as a hero.

A month later, the official victory parade saw the streets of Berlin festooned with flags and flowers, as Fritz and his cousin, Frederick Charles, rode immediately behind the King, proudly displaying their Field Marshal's batons. Never had the city resounded with such cries of victory, hailing the monarch who had left as a King and returned home as an Emperor.

Chapter 15 - The Crown Prince is an Imperialist

Throughout the long months away from home, the marches, the battles, the bloodshed and the siege, one thought had sustained Fritz: the certainty that victory would lead to unification. That outcome alone could make the whole bloody campaign worthwhile, and Napoleon's capitulation at Sedan convinced him that the time had come for his father to be proclaimed King of Germany.

Despite his irritation with Bismarck's interference in military tactics and his habit of parading around in uniform as though he were a serving soldier, Fritz was so determined to achieve that end that he offered to work with him to set the process in motion without delay. To his great disappointment, Bismarck failed to share his enthusiasm and phlegmatically replied that this was not the time for such drastic action, as the southern states had yet to be convinced of the merits of a Prussian-led empire. What was more, King William had so little interest in ruling an empire that he had forbidden any further discussion of the matter. Even the French were aware that the King and his son had opposing views, as Napoleon's friend, the Comtesse Mercy d'Argenteau, reported:

> "The Crown Prince is an Imperialist, and cares only for the Empire, of which he firmly believes Prussia will become the head. The King does not care for the Empire, and would prefer its chief to remain the King of Prussia, without any additional title to add to a glory which seems to him to be inherent to the dynasty of Hohenzollern."[201]

The other German Kings, said Bismarck, were equally sceptical about the merits of becoming a part of a German Empire. The King of Württemberg was concerned about the implications for his kingdom's autonomy; and had not King Ludwig obtained from Fritz an assurance of Bavaria's continued independence?

Unwilling to acknowledge the obstacles, Fritz replied that, as unification would eventually be inevitable, it was time to adopt a 'firm and commanding attitude' to bring the states into line. Bismarck merely smiled and reminded him that any attempt at coercion would drive them into the arms of Austria, potentially sparking another Austro-Prussian War.

Increasingly frustrated, Fritz persisted, suggesting that, when Bavaria and Württemberg saw that the other states were of one accord, they would realise they had no option but to follow their example; but Bismarck, unwilling to continue the conversation, impudently told him to say no more on that subject, as his views were contrary to those of his father.

> "I at once protested emphatically," Fritz recorded in his journal, "...that speech should not be denied to me in this way. Rather in such questions of the future, I regarded it as a duty not to leave any one in doubt as to my views; in any case, it rested with His Majesty alone to point out to me in what matters I might express myself, and in what not – if indeed I were not thought old enough to judge of them for myself."[202]

Taken aback, Bismarck churlishly huffed that, if his conduct were unsatisfactory, he would stand aside for anyone with whom the Crown Prince wished to replace him, but, until such a replacement was found, he must 'maintain his principles according to his best lights and individual knowledge of all the circumstances relating to the subject.'[203]

Fritz' temper instantly cooled, and, in a more conciliatory tone, he confessed he had spoken too hastily. He added, though, that he had been compelled to speak his mind because he wished to be involved in any decisions about the country's future.

Bismarck, with some justification, concluded that Fritz was more concerned about his own future position than about honouring his father's wishes; and, although the meeting ended with a modicum of courtesy, he privately remarked that the Crown Prince was 'vain' and 'stupid.'

As ever, Fritz was unaware that Bismarck had already embarked on a scheme of his own to bring the southern states into line. By arranging secret treaties with individual rulers, he hoped to buy their support for unification at a time of his choosing. He had given his word that the kings would retain much of their power and independence, and, in turn, they had agreed to pressurise King William into accepting the title of Emperor. Fritz' 'interference' threatened to scupper the plan, as it was widely known that he intended to curb the states' autonomy by subsuming them into one nation with a common foreign policy and constitution, headed by the King of Prussia, who would be known as King of the Germans.

Bismarck continued to weave his subtle web and, in mid-October 1870, as the German press clamoured for unification, ministers from Hesse, Baden and Württemberg visited King William at Versailles to discuss the situation. Within a month, Baden and Hesse had reached an agreement; and King Charles of Württemberg was on the point of so-doing when he heard that King Ludwig of Bavaria had arranged a meeting with the Austrian Chancellor. Suspecting that Bavaria was about to enter into an Austrian alliance, King Charles refused to make any agreement until he had discovered the details of King Ludwig's intentions.

In fact, as King Ludwig's overriding desire was to maintain his kingdom's independence, he was as reluctant to be dominated by Austria as he was to be ruled by Prussia. Rather than making a commitment to either side, he sent Bismarck a list of conditions which must be met before he would agree to support unification: he must retain full control of Bavarian domestic and foreign policy and maintain an independent Bavarian army; and, in return for his troops' contribution to the war, his territories should be expanded into Baden, for which the Grand Duke of Baden could be recompensed with an area in Alsace.

Disappointed by what he viewed as Fritz' betrayal, he sent his Prime Minister, Prince Chlodwig of Hohenlohe-Schillingsfürst, to visit Vicky in the hope that she would persuade her husband to rectify his error by accepting Bavarian demands. To his great disappointment, Prince Hohenlohe found that Vicky wholly supported Fritz' stance, and:

> "She was very dissatisfied about the convention with Bavaria but listened attentively to my defence of the special nature and justification of the Bavarian claims. It seemed to me that she and the Princess Alice did not care to recognise this preference shown to other German dynasties. Even with Saxony they were not satisfied. They are apparently enthusiastic upon the idea of a united empire without any exception, and do not like the proposal of federation."[204]

When Fritz heard of King Ludwig's demands, he was so incensed that he insisted that the Bavarians must be forced to submit, but Bismarck cunningly resorted instead to flattery. He thanked King Ludwig for his valuable assistance in the war and told him that, although the Grand Duke of Baden was not prepared to grant him land, if he were to visit Versailles, he and King William could discuss his demands in detail.

The eccentric Ludwig replied that he had sprained his ankle and it was too painful to travel, but he sent his uncle, Prince Luitpold, with an even more bizarre suggestion: he would incorporate his kingdom into a

German Empire on condition that the Imperial Crown should be shared between Prussia and Bavaria so that he and King William would take turns at acting as emperor.

"The King of Bavaria lives in a world of dreams," Bismarck retorted. "He is hardly more than a boy who does not know his own mind.'[205]

Nonetheless, he sent a respectful letter to Munich, agreeing that Bavaria could retain its own army, Minister of War and Foreign Minister; and he assured Ludwig that he would have the right to appoint his own diplomats and ambassadors. More importantly, he appealed directly to Ludwig's vanity, explaining that unification would happen with or without his support, but, if he were prepared to write to ask the King of Prussia to become emperor, he would be hailed as a hero all over Germany. If he refused to do so, that honour would be given to one of the lesser rulers, and he would be seen as having played no part in fulfilling the desires of the German people.

Ludwig was persuaded and, on 3rd December 1870, Bismarck read his letter to King William, which finally induced him to accept the inevitable. Fritz was overjoyed and, as he and Bismarck left the room, they shook hands warmly.

> "With today's work," Fritz recorded triumphantly in his diary, "Emperor and Empire are irrevocably established...this proud title is already pledged."[206]

The King certainly did not share his son's sense of triumph, as he gloomily complained to Queen Victoria that he had never wished to be anything other than King of Prussia and it was 'not without some regret' that he had to 'submit to an evident necessity.'[207] For several days, he refused to accept the need for a coronation or even an official proclamation of the German Empire; and, when at last he agreed to be crowned in Versailles on 18th January, he insisted that he would play no part in the preparations for the ceremony.

On the eve of the coronation, he caused greater consternation when he suddenly announced that he intended to be known as the Emperor of Germany. Bismarck tactfully reminded him that this would offend the other kings as it implied that he ruled their lands, which was not what they expected. Ultimately, he agreed to be named 'German Emperor'; Fritz would become an Imperial Highness; and Bismarck would be known as the Imperial Chancellor. In effort to raise his father's spirits, Fritz reminded him that Prussia had been evolving for centuries and the empire was a natural progression for a thriving nation.

"My son," said the King, "is with all his heart in the new order of things, while I care not a straw for them, and hold only by Prussia. I say that he and his successors are called to make the Empire now established into a reality."[208]

On the day of the coronation, the dreary weather reflected the King's gloom, and, as a consequence of the pouring rain, a planned procession had to be cancelled. Nonetheless, the ceremony took place in the Hall of Mirrors in Versailles with all the grandeur befitting so momentous an occasion. To rousing music, the rulers of the various states gathered in front of the colours of fifty-six regiments and, following a religious service, came the announcement of the re-establishment of the German Empire. Bismarck then read the proclamation to the nation.

"Long live His Imperial Majesty, Emperor William!' cried the Grand Duke of Baden; and, when the six hundred guests had repeated the refrain, Fritz, bursting with pride, genuflected before his father, whose tears flowed down his cheeks as he embraced him.

King William never fully accepted his new title or the idea of the German Empire. He continued to refer to his wife as the Queen rather than the Empress; and, although he diligently carried out his social and ceremonial duties, Prussia would always remain his priority.

Fritz, on the contrary, was so committed to the Empire that, even before the festivities were over, he lamented the fact that more stringent restrictions had not been placed on the other states. Their kings and princes, he complained, were an 'anachronistic impediment' to a unified nation:

> "To allow them to believe themselves indispensable factors in a situation which their pretensions only complicated to the detriment of its safety and welfare was…an error which should have been extinguished as soon as it was born."[209]

His zeal sprang not only from his desire to establish a national constitution but also from his genuine belief in Prussian superiority. Queen Victoria, who loved him deeply, observed that he shared the family trait of believing that all other dynasties were inferior to the Hohenzollerns; and another admirer described him as ambitious and 'deeply imbued with the characteristic greed of the Hohenzollerns. He would gladly have obliterated the other States out of which the whole fabric of the Empire was built.'[210]

Chapter 16 – 'I Am Accused of Taking No Interest In Public Affairs'

Optimism was in the air when Fritz returned triumphantly to Berlin in the spring of 1871. The war was won; the Empire was established; and, soon, workmen would begin removing the cobble stones and open drains to transform the city into a worthy capital for a unified Germany. In that moment of triumph, it must have seemed to Fritz, too, that his life was at a new beginning, as Bismarck had valued his support; and the adulation of his officers and men had boosted his self-confidence. Even his appearance matched his gallant reputation, as to many of his admirers he epitomised the ideal Teutonic hero – like the mythical knight, Lohengrin, so beloved by the less prepossessing King Ludwig of Bavaria.

> "Vivid still," one Englishman wrote, "remains the impression made upon me by the Crown Prince when for the first time I saw him approaching the tennis ground with his four Italian greyhounds, a splendid figure of dignified manhood, radiating kindliness with a friendly smile. One had only to see him to understand that his influence had been exerted, so far as his authority extended with his own army, on the side of humanity and in the defence of historic monuments during the war of '70."[211]

Unfortunately, the Prince of Wales, did not share his countryman's admiration, as the Franco-Prussian War had revived the old divisions between the brothers-in-law. An ardent Francophile, Bertie had been so critical of the German invasion of France that Queen Victoria, privately hoping for a Prussian victory, had insisted that he should not be informed of any news about the Germans' progress. Vicky dismissed her brother's complaints with the taunt that he was envious of her heroic husband, who, unlike Bertie, lived 'such a useful life.'

Yet again, Queen Victoria was forced to salve their relationship by inviting Fritz and Vicky to England in the hope of restoring harmony. When Bertie visited them at the German Embassy, he and Fritz were soon reconciled, and found common ground in their shared dislike of many of Bismarck's policies.

The brief collaboration between the Chancellor and the Crown Prince had ended almost as soon as the Empire was proclaimed. As a reward for his services, the Emperor had raised Bismarck to the rank of prince, and he relied upon him so heavily that his position became unassailable. This enabled him to mould Germany into his own ideal of a powerful nation, dismissing or destroying anyone who dared to oppose him. He fiercely berated the Reichstag for failing to support his policies; and he removed from office those who were unwilling to do his bidding.

> "He treated the Ambassadors that Germany held accredited at foreign Courts with a mixture of disdain and of rudeness that soon obliged them to resign, when they were immediately replaced by nonentities who never looked beyond humbly performing all the orders which they received from the Wilhelmstrasse, and who were so constantly told that they dared not take any personal initiative in anything that they lost it altogether."[212]

Even the Imperial Family was powerless to contradict him when the Emperor took his side in almost every disagreement. When the Empress criticised his draconian policies, the Emperor exclaimed, 'If she were not the Empress, I should spank her until she cried for mercy!'

The Empress was particularly aggrieved by Bismarck's decision to destroy the power of the Roman Catholic Church in Germany. His motives were neither religious nor ideological but rather political, as 'to be a

Catholic grew to seem synonymous with being a sympathizer with Austria and France.'[213]

In 1870, the Vatican declared the dogma of Papal Infallibility, which many of Germany's eight million Catholics feared would force them to place their allegiance to the Pope above their loyalty to the country. In a blatant show of disapproval, Bismarck appointed Cardinal Hohenlohe[z] – one of only four cardinals who had voted against the dogma – as German Ambassador to the Vatican. The Vatican protested so strongly that Hohenlohe was withdrawn but Bismarck ensured that no alternative was chosen to replace him. As the position remained vacant, relations between the Catholic hierarchy and Germany rapidly deteriorated, enabling Bismarck to institute a series of anti-clerical measures, which together became known as *Kulturkampf*.

In the summer of 1871, he abolished the Roman Catholic section of Ministry of Culture; and four months later, he forced the Pulpit Law through the Reichstag, making it a criminal offence to preach political sermons. The following year, the teaching of religion was banned in state schools, while Catholic schools were liable to regular inspections. The Jesuits Order, which was responsible for the greater part of Catholic education, was dissolved throughout Germany; and, in 1873, Bismarck claimed the right to interfere in ecclesiastical appointments and made it illegal for any priest who had not been educated in Germany to be given a position. Clergymen who spoke out against the regime were sent into exile, and those who deliberately flouted the law were imprisoned.

In his own defence, Bismarck stated honestly that he had no personal grudge against any denomination but he aimed to ensure that German Catholics shared 'all the

---

[z] The Cardinal was the brother of Prince Chlodwig Hohenlohe, the Prime Minister of Bavaria.

religious liberties enjoyed by other German subjects compatible with the laws of the empire and secondly to arrest the anti-national political intrigues of a certain portion of the ultramontanes[aa] in Poland and elsewhere.'[214]

When the Empress, who had many Catholic friends, warned that the measures would lead to revolution, Bismarck resorted to his usual tactic of smearing her in the press while convincing the Emperor that she was losing her reason.

> "Prince Bismarck," the wife of the British Ambassador wrote to Queen Victoria, "often expresses his hatred for the Empress in such strong language that my husband is placed in a very difficult position…Prince Bismarck being so unscrupulous in his use of the press to undermine his political enemies – as his letter insinuating that the Empress was sending to the refractory Catholic priests…proves."[215]

Fritz's main concern was that *kulturkampf* was creating unnecessary discord, and risked destabilising the Empire. His supporters urged him to speak out against the measures but he remained silent, and the consequent criticism, wounded him deeply.

"I am accused of taking no interest in public affairs," he sighed to a friend, "and the party in power take care that I am never informed on them."[216]

His increasingly disillusioned supporters were less than convinced by his claim, as they observed that, when he *was* invited to participate in affairs of state, he appeared too lethargic make any useful contributions. During meetings of the Council of Ministers, 'he almost dislocated his jaw with yawning, and gradually stopped going'[217]; and when he was invited to contribute to a discussion, he replied, 'I beg to be excused from expressing an opinion.'

[aa] Ultramontanism = the strong belief in the authority of the pope.

To many of his erstwhile supporters, the hero of Sedan and Koniggrätz was tumbling from his pedestal, as he, who had been so courageous in wartime, now seemed to contribute nothing to the running of the Empire. Others suggested he was biding his time until he became Emperor, leading his critics to conclude that, 'he thought it unfair of Providence to let his father live so long'[218]

The Emperor virtually ignored him; Bismarck excluded from his plans; and his relationship with his mother was rapidly deteriorating. As time passed, the Empress had become increasingly resentful of Vick's happy marriage and the simple fact that he daughter-in-law was younger than she was. Having once been a beautiful woman, she:

> "...could not resign herself to growing old gracefully. She would have made a most charming old lady, but though well over seventy then, she was ill-advised enough to attempt to rejuvenate herself with a chestnut wig and an elaborate make-up, with deplorable results. The Empress, in addition, was afflicted with a slight palsy of the head."[219]

Taking out her frustration and resentment on Fritz, she publicly scolded him when arrived fifteen minutes early for the Emperor's birthday, and left him standing like a schoolboy outside the door. She made point, too, of appearing at every function that he and Vicky attended, solely to ensure that she, not they, gained the most attention.

> "She's so skinny now that her old bones fairly rattle," Fritz gasped in exasperation, "But that does not keep her at home. She must put in an appearance even though she's got one foot in the grave."[220]

His father, meanwhile, continued to control him by limiting his allowance and, as he sighed that he might have to give up hunting at Spandau because it was so expensive, he was irked to see that Bismarck was regularly lavished with luxurious gifts. 'My future subject has a private railway-carriage and I have not!' he declared; and on another occasion he remarked, 'He is given an order in diamonds, and I am not!'[221]

His frustration made him despondent and led to regular bouts of ill-health, exacerbated by depression. In 1872, while staying in Dresden for the King and Queen of Saxony's Golden Wedding anniversary celebrations he caught a cold which led to a recurrence of the inflammatory illness that had laid him low during the Franco-Prussian War. When the celebrations were over, he set out to meet Vicky in Switzerland but, on reaching Karlsruhe, he became so ill that his doctors feared he was dying. Vicky desperately hurried to be with him, and was overjoyed when she arrived on 26th November, to find he was beginning to recover.

> "We have been on the threshold of a great misfortune," wrote the British military commissioner. "The Crown Prince has been seriously ill. At one time there was real danger, which, thank God, has now passed…It is terrible to think the hindrance to the consolidation of Germany which would ensue from the death of the Crown Prince."[222]

Bismarck, too, was greatly relieved to hear of his recovery, as he believed that the aging Emperor did not have long to live. His frailty was becoming more apparent and there were many at court who suspected that he was in the early stages of dementia as he showed symptoms similar to those that had afflicted his brother, Frederick William IV.

> "The Emperor's intellect began to work less easily," Bismarck observed; "he had difficulty in comprehending what others said and in developing

his own statements; at times he lost the thread in listening and speaking."[223]

Driven by personal ambition and the desire to consolidate all that he had achieved, Bismarck was determined to retain his position when the Emperor died. Although he knew that Vicky despised him, he believed that Fritz saw him as the only minister capable of shaping the newly-unified Empire and that he would not 'allow himself to be ruled by his wife'[224] regarding his choice of Chancellor.

He would have been gratified to know that, while he was considering his future, Fritz was also contemplating his importance to the Empire. His illness led him to think of what would happen if he and his father should die before his eldest son reached his majority, and, as Vicky would almost certainly be appointed as regent, he asked her to promise to retain Bismarck's services if ever such a situation should arise.

Meanwhile, Fritz' eldest daughter, Charlotte, was developing from an awkward child into a difficult young woman. Floating the through the New Palace in such a cloud of tobacco that she smelt 'like a walking cigar box', her moods swung from apathy to inexplicable rages.

> "She was," wrote her cousin, Marie of Edinburgh, "...one of the most fickle and changeable women I have ever had to do with....Charly belonged to those beings who, with a single word of disdain, could shrivel up your ardent enthusiasm, make your dearest possession appear worthless or rob your closest friend of her charm, and this with a voice, soft and gentle like a caress."[225]

By the age of sixteen she had become so flirtatious that her mother feared she would cause a major scandal; and it came almost as a relief when she suddenly announced that she wished to marry her father's cousin,

Prince Bernhard of Saxe-Meiningen. Although taken aback by the news, Fritz was not unduly concerned, as Bernhard was a fine officer with a distinguished record in the Franco-Prussian War, and a sensible husband, nine years her senior, might help to calm his wayward daughter.

The engagement was announced in 1877; and, although gossips claimed that Charlotte was only marrying to escape from her mother's clutches, Fritz and Vicky were delighted by Bernhard's obvious devotion to her.

They were married in a double wedding with Prince Frederick Charles' daughter, Elizabeth, and a Prince of Oldenburg, in February 1878; and Queen Victoria sent two of her sons, the Prince of Wales and the Duke of Connaught[bb], to represent her at the ceremony.

"Vicky and Fritz are most blooming," the Prince of Wales reported. "It is impossible to find two nicer boys than William and Henry, and they are continually with us for Fritz and Vicky have so much to do."[226]

Less effusively, Vicky told the Queen that the wedding 'went off very well' before lamenting the gap in her household left by her daughter's departure.

It was only a matter of time before she and Fritz faced a second wrench, as their son, Henry, completed his naval training and prepared to embark on a two-year round-the-world voyage. Terrified for his safety, Vicky pleaded with the Emperor to excuse him, but her father-in-law replied that his grandson had a duty to brave the same dangers as any other seaman.

When Henry had left, Fritz and Vicky set out for England, where Fritz visited a series of industrial sites and was warmly received by the workers. On 11th May, he received a telegram from Berlin, informing that his sister

---

[bb] At the wedding, the Duke of Connaught met and fell in love with Elizabeth's sister, Louise Margaret, whom he married the following year.

and father had been riding in a 'victoria'[cc] when a handyman named Max Hödel fired a shot at them. Neither the Emperor nor his daughter was hurt but a bullet killed a bystander, and when Hödel was arrested and charged with treason, he claimed that he had been trying to commit suicide. The unlikely story was quickly discredited when witnesses attested that he had bragged that he would soon be famous.

At the end of the month, as Queen Victoria migrated to Scotland, Fritz and Vicky remained in London at the home of the Prince of Wales. On 2nd June, they visited Lord Beaconsfield[dd] at Hatfield House, from where they took a trip with Lord and Lady Salisbury to neighbouring Pashanger House, the home of the Earl of Cowper. Their carriage had only just arrived when an aide, Major von Panwitz, came galloping up behind them with ominous news from Prussia.

The eighty-one-year-old Emperor had been travelling along the Unter den Linden when a socialist, Karl Nobiling, fired at him from a double-barrelled shotgun. Thirty pellets punctured his arms, face and neck, causing such profuse bleeding that he briefly lost consciousness, but, when he came round, he gave orders to send for Fritz without delay.

Fritz and Vicky hastened back to Hatfield, from where they caught a train to London, and, two hours later, they boarded a ship at Dover. The next day, Fritz arrived in Berlin to find his father looking so pale and frail that he might have been dying; and the doctors warned that, although in a younger man none of the wounds would have been life-threatening, in view of the Emperor's age, they could not guarantee a full recovery. Aware that, if he survived, he would need a long period of recuperation, the

---

[cc] A type of open carriage.
[dd] The Prime Minister, Benjamin Disraeli, was created Lord Beaconsfield in 1876.

Emperor appointed Fritz as regent but added that he must allow Bismarck to make all political decisions.

This stipulation severely limited Fritz' power, but he took the opportunity of lessening the friction between Germany and the Vatican by beginning a conciliatory correspondence with the Pope, despite the complaints of the hard-line protestants. On the second day of the regency, he also angered the Junkers by appointing his Jewish friend, Heinrich von Friedberg to the prestigious post of Minister of Justice. Friedberg had extensive experience in various judicial posts but, until then, his chances of promotion had always been hindered by an undercurrent of anti-Semitism.

Fritz was powerless, though, to prevent the Chancellor from using the attack on the Emperor as a means of forcing through his political agenda. After Hödel's assassination attempt, he had tried to suppress the Social Democrats – a party from which Hödel had been expelled eight years earlier – by prohibiting meetings and banning their publications, but the Reichstag had rejected his efforts. Nobiling's more serious assault gave him an excuse to dissolve the Reichstag and call an election, which, he hoped, would return more reactionary members, who would support his harsher measures.

In July, his gamble paid off when a significant number of socialists lost their seats, which enabled him to draw up a Bill 'for the protection of the State and of Society from the dangers threatened by the excesses of the Social Democrats.'[227] The Bill passed through the Reichstag with a substantial majority, paving the way for Bismarck to enact a series of oppressive laws throughout the next decade.

Only one important task fell to Fritz during the brief regency: he was required to authorise the execution of Max Hödel. After seriously wounding the Emperor, Nobiling had shot himself in the head and remained in a coma from which he would never recover; but Hödel had been sentenced to death by beheading. Fritz, who had found war repugnant, was distraught at the thought that his signature would lead to the decapitation of a 'mental defective' but the law was the law and he was powerless to change it. When the prisoner was executed on 16th August, Fritz sighed to a friend that he had never felt more unhappy than when he had signed the document that sent a man to his death.

Contrary to all expectations, the Emperor rapidly regained his strength and, by December, he had not only made a full recovery but, miraculously, was more mentally alert than ever.

> "Curiously enough," wrote Bismarck, "a change for the better began after Nobiling's attempt on his life…The Emperor was freer, had more life, and was also more easily moved. When I expressed my delight at the good state of his health he was moved to the jest, 'Nobiling knew better than the doctors what I wanted – a good letting of blood.'"[228]

The regency ended and, as his services were no longer required, Fritz was again relegated to the side-lines, taking comfort from the fact that his father allowed Friedberg to retained his position despite complaints from several ministers.

Chapter 17 – Pain, Deep and Cruel Beyond Words

On 14th December 1878, the seventeenth anniversary of the death of Price Albert, Vicky received a black-edged telegram, informing her of the death of her thirty-five-year-old sister, Alice. Diphtheria had spread through Alice's Grand Duchy of Hesse-Darmstadt, striking her children and husband one after another. Alice had bravely nursed them herself, and all but one of her children recovered, but, exhausted and depressed, she, too, succumbed to the disease in early December.

Vicky was inconsolable, as she and Alice had always been close, sharing a bedroom as children and, later, comparing their experiences of married life in Germany. They had supported one another through the upheavals of the Franco-Prussian War; and, much to the horror of Queen Victoria, they had even breast-fed each other's babies.

Fritz was deeply upset that his father refused to allow him and Vicky to attend the funeral for fear that they would bring the infection back to Prussia. Vicky complained to her mother that the decision 'jarred greatly on our feelings and made us very unhappy'[229]; and the British press expressed disgust at the Emperor's 'cruel and cowardly' decision.

The Emperor's precautions proved futile as the disease soon spread to Berlin, and, in mid-March 1879, eleven-year-old Waldemar began to show symptoms. The highly-infectious disease, known to the Spanish as 'the strangler', attacks the lymph nodes in the throat, causing the membranes to swell across the tonsils and, eventually, across the airways. As the sufferer slowly asphyxiates, toxins spread through the body to the liver and kidneys causing complete organ failure, leading to a painful and horrific death.

Fritz remained optimistic as most of Alice's children had recovered, and the doctors assured him that his son had only a mild version of the illness. Vicky insisted on nursing him herself, taking the necessary precautions: donning protective clothing before she approached his bed; and spraying herself with disinfectant before leaving the room.

'The dear patient is not in an unsatisfactory state,'[230] she wrote to Queen Victoria on 25th March, although Waldemar's tonsil was as large as a walnut, and he was in intense pain with great difficulty in swallowing. The next day, she remained hopeful, informing her mother that 'the doctors feel quite cheerful about him but of course all cause for anxiety is not over yet!'[231]

That night, his condition suddenly deteriorated and at half-past-eleven, a specialist, Dr Langenbeek, was urgently summoned. Sadly, there was nothing that Langenbeek could do, and at three-thirty in the morning of 26th March, Waldemar's heart gave out and he gasped his last. 'With a trembling hand,' Vicky informed her mother that 'the nicest and most promising of my boys is gone.'[232]

'The grief of my parents for the loss of this splendid son was unspeakable;' wrote William, 'our pain deep and cruel beyond words.'[233]

Four days later, the funeral took place in the Friedenskirche in Potsdam. Mountains of floral tributes filled the chapel, including wreathes of camelias from Vicky's family, and bouquets from across the whole of Germany. Cannon boomed across the town and bells tolled in all the churches as the pastor spoke warmly of Waldemar's many talents, and his hope that the grieving parents might find comfort in their faith and in one another. When the congregation rose to leave, Fritz dropped to his knees beside the catafalque, kissing the pall that draped the white coffin.

"Then, endeavouring to compose himself," the British press reported, "he approached his Royal mother and sister and assisted them tenderly from their bended knees. After the mourners had left the church, his Highness returned for a moment with the weeping mother, [and] both the afflicted parents muttered a broken prayer over the remains of their son before they were finally deposited beside the ashes of Prince Sigismund, cut off also in the very budding-time of life."[234]

While much of the country mourned with Fritz, Bismarck callously and discourteously refused to cancel a soirée that he had arranged that evening, and, as Fritz left the Friedenskirche, the Chancellor was cheerfully entertaining a large group of politicians as though nothing untoward had happened.

In deepest mourning, Fritz and his family withdrew to the spa town of Wiesbaden, but, a few months later, their spirits lifted at the birth of their first grandchild[ee]. In the autumn, there was further good news when William was betrothed to Princess Victoria Augusta Victoria ('Dona'), the eldest daughter of Duke Frederick of Schleswig-Holstein-Augustenburg

Vicky predicted that, in view of Dona's relatively lowly status, the public would be unenthusiastic about the match, but she and Fritz appreciated the princess's docility and they believed that marriage would be good for William. Bismarck was so pleased by the engagement, which he hoped would stifle the lingering anti-Prussian sentiments in Schleswig-Holstein, that he took the unusual step of attending the official betrothal ceremony on 2nd June 1880.

As Vicky had foreseen, members of the extended family were far less appreciative, and the public appeared

---

[ee] Charlotte had given birth to a daughter, Feodore.

indifferent to the future bride. When Dona made her official entry into Berlin, one witness observed that:

> "Every face wore an expression of curiosity, but not of enthusiasm or delight, for the marriage was not a popular one...The young bride...wore a white and pink gown, and a diadem on her fair hair. She bowed right and left, while the people stared and a few shrill cheers were to be heard. I remember that we all agreed in thinking her very insignificant, and a general opinion prevailed that love had been the least factor in bringing about the union."[235]

William, however, was very popular in Berlin, and, when he rode out at the head of his regiment the cheering erupted. He escorted his wife to the old Schloss where Fritz offered her his arm and led her to the Swiss Hall to be greeted by a gathering of his extended family. Unfortunately, they, too, gave her a lukewarm reception, prompting Fritz to complain 'of the unfriendliness with which the betrothal had been received by the other Prussian princes and princesses."[236]

The wedding took place on 27th February 1881, followed by lengthy celebrations which Fritz and Vicky found 'exhausting, suffocating and interminable.' William, though, was obviously happy, and for the rest of her life, he and Dona would remain devoted to one another. Over the next decade, she gave birth to six sons and a daughter, leaving no one in any doubt that William had secured the Hohenzollern dynasty.

Two weeks after the wedding, Berlin was rocked by the dramatic news that Tsar Alexander II had had been travelling from a meeting at the Mikhailovsky Palace in St Petersburg when a nihilist bomb exploded beneath his carriage. He emerged unharmed but, as he stepped out to help his wounded attendants, a second attacker hurled another bomb, shattering his legs and ripping open his abdomen. He was rushed back to his palace where he died soon afterwards.

Fritz hastened to Russia as his father's representative at the funeral, but he had barely left home when Vicky received an anonymous letter warning that he would be murdered in St Petersburg. The letter arrived at the moment that she was returning from a service for Waldemar's anniversary, and, although it was obviously a hoax, it was hurtful to know that it was designed purely to distress her.

Fritz returned unharmed but the Tsar's death and the attempts on his father's life, had left him with a morbid awareness of his own mortality. He became convinced that he was about to be assassinated, telling his friend Friedberg, 'Whenever I get out of my coach I wonder whether the shot will come from the right or from the left.'[237] Only a few months later, he had a narrow escape from a potentially fatal accident when he was travelling on a fast train on the Berlin and Potsdam railway. A carriage was stuck on a level crossing, as the horses had taken fright and fled, and fled, and, were it not for the swift thinking of the driver, there was no doubt that the train would have hit the obstacle at speed and been derailed.

Bismarck, meanwhile, used the Tsar's assassination as another excuse to crush the socialists, whom he described as 'vermin' in need of extermination. To lessen support for their policies, he introduced a series of welfare measures in the hope that the public would no longer see any need for socialism. As his policies were to be introduced over several years, he expected the Emperor to die before his programme was completed. Knowing he would need the support of his successor, he arranged several meetings with Fritz to involve him in plans for workers' health insurance, protection for those injured at work, and eventually old age pensions.

Fritz might have hoped that Bismarck's desire for his cooperation demonstrated a shift in the statesman's attitude towards him but he was soon to be disillusioned. It came as a great blow to him when Bismarck decided that, in view of his anti-Russian sentiments, it would be inappropriate for him to attend the Tsar's coronation in May 1883, and he persuaded the Emperor to send William instead. Vicky was so angry that, when her son returned from Russia, she refused to allow him even to mention the visit; and Fritz was indignant to think, while William had been fraternising with grand dukes and princes, he had been relegated to attending the celebrations for the four-hundredth birthday of Martin Luther.

That autumn, however, he was given a more prestigious assignment: a visit to Madrid for a meeting with King Alfonso XII of Spain. Alfonso had recently visited Berlin to discuss a potential defensive treaty between Germany and Spain; and it was hoped that Fritz' return visit would allow for further discussions of the subject. Delighted by the prospect of a meeting with the Spanish King, whom he described as the most intelligent sovereign he had ever known, Fritz anticipated the trip with excitement and enthusiasm but, when he mentioned that Vicky would be accompanying him, Bismarck indignantly replied that the Emperor would not allow it.

Once again, at the age of fifty-two, Fritz had been treated like a child, and further humiliation followed when, shortly before his departure, he was told that he must be accompanied by a detective named Kruger. Convinced that Kruger was Bismarck's spy, Fritz bristled with indignation but, in fact, unbeknown to him, the detective had been appointed in response to a warning from London of socialist plot to assassinate him during the visit. Also accompanying him were four journalists, selected by Vicky's private secretary, Karl von Normann. A fierce critic of Bismarck, Normann naively believed that the journalists would write a comprehensive account of his travels, to prevent the Chancellor from claiming the credit for the success of his visit.

His first port of call was Genoa, where, in spite of the lateness of the hour, huge crowds turned out to greet him to thank him for the funds he had raised for the earthquake victims of Ischia[ff]. An equally warm welcome awaited him in Madrid on 23rd November, when he rode with King Alfonso to the Royal Palace. The young King, who had ascended the throne nine years earlier at the age of only seventeen, warned Fritz that his ministry would not sanction any formal agreement despite his eagerness to secure good relations with Germany. Nonetheless, the two men gave 'verbal assurances of mutual assistance moral support at first, but then, according to circumstances, material support as well in case either of the two countries we represent should be threatened by the French.'[238] Beyond their discussion, the King had arranged a series of tours and entertainments, and Fritz spent a fortnight visiting historic sites and the local museums.

He had planned to continue his journey to Lisbon to pay his respects to the King of Portugal, but, shortly before his departure, he received a message from Berlin, telling him to return instead to Italy. In his determination to crush the socialists, Bismarck sought Catholic allies, and he hoped that a visit to the Vatican would be seen by German Catholics as a gesture of reconciliation. Although 'flabbergasted' by the request, Fritz felt obliged to comply because, as Vicky wrote to her mother, 'it was decreed by Jupiter from Olympian Heights.'[239]

On 22nd December, Fritz arrived in Rome for a pleasant reunion with an old friend, King Umberto, who arranged for him to attend several military reviews. Much to the surprise of the world's press, he was granted an audience with Pope Leo XIII, which turned out to be a

---

[ff] See Chapter 18

cause of great embarrassment. The Pope assumed that the Emperor or Bismarck had sent him with a specific message and, as Fritz said nothing substantial, he could not understand the purpose of the visit. Nonetheless, to conceal his humiliation, Fritz later tried to portray the meeting as having been worthwhile:

> "Being the guest of the King of Italy, I have also been able to pay a visit to the Pope. These are facts of great importance, of which our country will reap the benefit."[240]

By the time that he returned home, he was still seething about the instruction to return via Italy, and the pointless and awkward meeting with the Pope. Although the order had officially come from his father, he understood that it was at Bismarck's bidding, and, in giving a full report of his trip to the Foreign Secretary, he angrily added that:

> "…He really would appreciate it if on future occasions the Chancellor and his entourage would see that he, the Crown Prince, was not chivvied around again so aimlessly. It was not his job to chase across the globe as Prince Bismarck's courier…His one surprise in Rome was that no further instructions came telling him to go to Bucharest immediately. Nor had the Chancellor briefed him for his audience with the Pope, as if he meant to say, it doesn't really matter if you put your foot in it."[241]

His fraught relationship with Bismarck intensified when the four journalists reported all that he had said in unguarded moments, illustrating the growing mistrust between him and the Chancellor.

Chapter 18 – Fits of Gloom & Depression

In the summer of 1882, Emperor William's only surviving brother, Charles, slipped while ascending a staircase, fracturing his femur. For several weeks, he was confined to bed and, as he began to recover, it was clear that the shock had left him frailer and more prone to infection. In January 1883, while taking the air in his gardens, he developed a cold that quickly progressed into pneumonia.

When he died on 21st January, the British press reported the 'sad' event most deferentially, but Fritz and Vicky had little reason to mourn a man whom they had viewed as 'wicked' and even 'a monster.' They were far more concerned that his passing disrupted their plans for their Silver Wedding anniversary celebrations, which were due to take place four days later. 'Even in his death,' Vicky remarked, 'the Prince was still unfriendly, for by dying at that time he stopped all the arrangements for a bright and joyful event.'[242]

Although the public festivities were postponed, the Emperor gave permission for the family celebrations to continue as planned, and so, on 25th January, guests gathered in the flower-bedecked New Palace, bearing so many gifts that there was barely time to view them. The Emperor had promised to give the couple a gift of money but, much to Fritz' annoyance, he asked him to negotiate an appropriate amount with two civil servants. Fritz was most put out by the civil servants' 'intrusion into his daily affairs' and, although he expressed gratitude, he added that neither he nor Vicky would discuss their finances with anyone outside the family.

Nonetheless, on the day of the celebrations, the slight was forgiven and, when the Emperor and Empress arrived shortly before noon, they presented Vicky and Fritz with a Chinese tea service in solid silver. Queen Victoria, who was represented the Duke and Duchess of Edinburgh, sent a bust of herself, created by the renowned sculptor Jacob Boehm; Vicky's brothers had commissioned a copy of a painting of the daughters of George III; and, among several other art works that they received was a portrait of their eldest son dressed in Highland costume. William himself gave his parents a Louis XIV writing desk; and dignitaries and friends sent numerous pieces of silver. The most impressive gift came from the members of the household: a beautifully decorated Sechstein grand piano.

"On the inside of the lid," the *Times* reported, "is painted the gala equipage, drawn by three pairs of horses in gorgeous trappings, in which they made their public entry into Berlin; and the panels contain paintings of Balmoral, Windsor, the New Palace, scenes from the Riviera and other places intimately associated with their married life."[243]

A few weeks later, the postponed public celebrations took place, including an Elizabeth pageant and performances from artistes from across the continent. Municipalities donated vast sums of money to a fund that Fritz and Vicky established to be shared between charities for orphans, widows and the poor; and the establishment of a new nursing institution for wounded soldiers. Five months later, Fritz launched a further appeal on behalf of the people of Ischia, where an earthquake had left three-thousand people dead and many thousands more with serious injuries.

Newspaper accounts of the celebrations created an image of a happy, united family but, beneath the veneer, discord permeated the household. Fritz was aware of a growing rift between Vicky and his advisor, Normann; he was still annoyed that William had been sent to the Tsar's coronation; and he was irked by the Emperor's decision to move his second son, Henry, from the navy to the army. When the family performed a play in honour of the anniversary, Charlotte deliberately spoiled the event by repeatedly upstaging and ridiculing her sister-in-law, Dona. Clearly, marriage and motherhood had done nothing to improve her behaviour, and, as soon as her daughter was born, she had declared she would have no more children and promptly returned to her fashionable friends, her extravagant lifestyle and her foreign holidays.

"The great love of amusement is much to be regretted," a shocked Queen Victoria wrote to Vicky, "and then I blame her husband very much if he allows what you say?"[244]

Still more disconcerting was the rapid deterioration of William's relationship with Vicky. Several observers concluded that mother and son were 'temperamentally too much alike ever to get on'[245]; and Queen Victoria's Private Secretary remarked that, 'There are faults on both sides. How are these to be got rid of?'[246]

Under the influence of Bismarck and the Emperor, William had come to believe that his mother placed British interests above those of Germany; while Vicky was irked her to see how the Berliners loved William at a time when Fritz was becoming more unpopular.

"In Berlin the Crown Prince was not liked," one observer later reported, "and, placed as he was between an old father who had become the idol of the German nation and a young son in whom that nation saw a future conqueror as well as a great man, he had bitterly felt the disagreeable conditions of this anomalous situation and resented it, perhaps more than he ought to have done."[247]

Unfavourable comparisons between Fritz and William were not confined to Germany, for, as far away at the United States, it was reported that:

"The Prince William...is intelligent, brave, hot headed, but with a 'heart of gold,' sympathetic, impulsive, vivacious, popular with all classes...He is the most successful of the Hohenzollerns, and more popular than his scholarly father, the Crown Prince, who, it is said, has cold manners, and cannot readily come to a decision, and is thought to be too much under the rule of his wife, the dominant Princess Victoria of England."[248]

Although Fritz was greatly loved in Britain, across much of the rest of Europe he was viewed as insignificant, and devoid of ideas beyond the ambition to rule. One French commentator joked that his opponents need not worry about what changes he would make on his accession, as he was too irresolute ever to reach a decision:

"Ses manières sont froides; malgré sa bonne grâce, on ne se sent pas à l'aise avec lui. Il a de la familiarité plus que de la bienveillance. Son cœur est vraiment bon, mais ses détracteurs prétendent qu'il ne parviendra pas à conquérir une plus grande situation comme souverain qu'il n'a su en conquérir une comme héritier du trône."[gg][249]

Although William had no control over what foreign journalists chose to write, the articles confirmed Vicky's belief that her son was deliberately trying to usurp his father's position. When Fritz was away in Italy and Spain, she bitterly observed that that William visited his grandfather every day; and, rather than seeking his parents' permission to undertake various duties or journeys, he dealt directly with the Emperor. Although she reluctantly conceded that it was more convenient for William to consult his grandfather than to speak with his absent father, she complained to Queen Victoria that:

[gg] 'His manner is cold; in spite of his good grace one never feels at ease with him. He has more familiarity than benevolence. His heart is truly good but his detractors His heart is really good, but his detractors claim that he never will not be able to conquer the greater position as sovereign as he could conquer that of heir to the throne.'

"We are not even informed of what they mean to do…It is most painful and disagreeable."[250]

With each passing month, the dispute between Vicky and William became more obvious. She grumbled that he failed to ask after her health when she was suffering from an eye complaint, and, in return, she refused to join a toast to him on his birthday. When Fritz and William were alone, their relationship was more harmonious but, as William told a friend, when his mother was present, 'the wind blows in a different direction.'

Fritz himself, however, made no secret of his preference for his younger son, Henry, as one experienced officer observed when the two young men had joined their father on manoeuvres:

> "The fact that Prince William has been summoned to headquarters, which means to join his father, was completely ignored. The Crown Prince never once asked me, 'Where is my son?' or 'What is he doing?' When the latter, as constantly happened in the course of the manoeuvres, returned to my headquarters, his father behaved as if he scarcely knew he was there, but took much notice of Prince Henry, who was on his staff. Prince William, however, allowed no one to see how much he felt this unfriendliness from his father."[251]

On another occasion, when an American diplomat, complimented William, Fritz replied without hesitation, 'Yes, he's a fine lad, but you should see my boy Henry!'[252]

Ironically, following Fritz' controversial speech in Danzig[hh], his father had accused him of trying to establish a rival court; and now Fritz levelled the same accusation at his own eldest son. Although neither allegation was true, two distinct factions were beginning to form: one around

---

[hh] See Chapter 8

the Emperor, Bismarck and William; and the other around Fritz and Vicky.

The former group, which included the diplomat, Holstein, General von Abedyll and Field Marshal Waldersee, despised Vicky and viewed Fritz as weak, easily-manipulated and apathetic.

"The intellectual superiority of the Princess has proved a great misfortune," Waldersee claimed. "She has turned a simple-minded, gallant, honourable Prince into a weak-minded man devoid of self-reliance, no longer open-hearted, no longer Prussian in his ideas. Even of his steadfast faith she has robbed him...If the Emperor lives much longer, the Crown Prince will go to pieces altogether. Even as it is, he has attacks of profound depression, and no confidence in the future."[253]

The more deeply Fritz sank into depression, the more outspoken Vicky became, which in turn prompted her enemies to attack her more venomously. 'When the Crown Prince comes to power,' the Foreign Minister remarked, 'the Crown Princess will be Kaiser.'[254]

'The Crown Princess actually hates Germany and the Germans, and says so quite often,' Holstein wrote in his diary, and he was constantly seeking evidence to support his spurious claim. She refused to help a German art school purchase a series of paintings, which she believed should remain in England; and the British Foreign Secretary, Lord Rosebery, was alleged to have told the Prince of Wales that she had inflamed the whole of Germany against England by her 'foolish and incessant flaunting of her English nationality.'[255]

Most damaging of all for Vicky was an 'anonymous' pamphlet, which everyone knew was written by her uncle, the Duke of Saxe-Coburg and Gotha. Entitled *Co-Regents and Foreign Influence in Germany*, the treatise accused her of indiscretion, disloyalty, and too great a dependence on her mother. It was circulated widely through Germany, Austria and Russia, and created such a sensation that Fritz' critics suggested that, when the Emperor died, the throne should pass directly to his grandson.

The faction that formed around Fritz and Vicky, was equally mischievous in creating discord within the family. William's achievements were dismissed as attempts to court public approval, and he was accused of using his popularity in Berlin to divert attention away from his father. Misinterpreting the natural bond between William and the Emperor, they 'took advantage of certain facts...to turn them to their own profit, and went from one person to another carrying tales, mostly construed out of their personal, generally false, impressions, which not only did considerable harm, but also brought about a complete misunderstanding.'[256]

Relations became so tense that, rather than seeking a reconciliation, Fritz tried to place tighter controls on William's activities.

"The Crown Prince," complained Holstein, "who after all knows what it feels like to be too strictly held in check, is now treating his son in exactly the same way as he himself was treated."[257]

In an effort to ease the tension, Fritz arranged for William to leave Berlin with his regiment but, when the Emperor heard what was happening, he refused to allow him to go. Vicky complain bitterly to her mother that her son and father-in-law were 'in the hands of very unprincipled and violent people.'[258]

Regardless of Fritz' protestations, the Emperor continued to give orders directly to William without first consulting his parents about his plans. Fritz was incensed when William told him that the Emperor was sending him to meet the Tsar at Skierniewice in Poland, and he wrote a strongly-worded letter to Bismarck expressing his objections to the plan. Bismarck calmly replied that the Tsar had already been informed of the arrangements and, therefore, they could not be altered. When William heard of his father's annoyance, he sent him an uncoded telegram, pointing out that he was acting on the Emperor's instructions:

> "As regards your observation on my failure to inform the New Palace of my plans for travelling to S[kierniewice], I asked His Majesty's permission twice because I foresaw what would happen but he required me on my word of honour not to say a word to anyone."[259]

Furious that the telegraph operators had been able to read the communication, Fritz hastily prepared a letter for the Tsar, explaining that his son was in delicate health and, as he not well enough to travel, he himself would replace him. He sent the letter to Bismarck, in the hope that he would forward it to Skierniewice, but, rather than so doing, he showed it to the Emperor, who replied that William had already established a rapport with the Tsar and he did not believe the excuse that he was unfit for the journey.

Fritz was forced to yield and, a few days later, he heard that William was to be given a placement in the Foreign Office. Again, he picked up his pen and wrote to the Emperor:

> "In view of the immaturity as well as the inexperience of my eldest son, together with his tendency towards overbearingness and self-conceit, I cannot but frankly regard it as dangerous to allow him at present to take any part in foreign affairs."[260]

The Emperor ignored his objections, and, when Fritz complained that William should obey him because a father had a right to expect obedience from his son, Bismarck coldly replied that 'in the royal family the paternal authority must yield to the monarchical.'

Fritz came to the gloomy conclusion that the powerful triumvirate of his father, William and Bismarck were planning not only to remove him from the succession but also to write him out history altogether. He became even more convinced that there was a plot afoot to kill him, as the Minister of Justice reported: 'The Crown Prince...believes that an attempt on his life is being planned. In other respects, also he is dissatisfied.'[261]

In despair, he contemplated abdicating and allowing the throne to pass directly from the Emperor to William.

"In recent years," wrote Holstein, "the Prince has had fits of gloom and depression, the causes of which can be summed up by saying he regards himself as a 'defeated point of view'. It is gradually dawning on him that the Liberal regime he had hoped to establish would not now ensure him general popularity. He intended to rule with and for the bourgeoisie, and is thrown into perplexity by the more rapid emergence of the workers...Sometimes he even talks of abdicating his claims – an idea he will never act upon as long as [Vicky] is alive."[262]

Even within his home, divisions were becoming apparent as Vicky's private secretary, Normann, appeared to have turned against her. Formerly, he had only dealt with Fritz via Vicky, but now he was ignoring her to deal with him directly. 'The intention of influencing the husband without, or against, his wife was evident in all N[ormann] said,' one diplomat reported; and rumours began to spread that all was not well within Fritz' marriage. It was alleged that Vicky had raged at him for employing a coachman whom she did not like; and that he was always depressed because he was afraid to contradict her. Although there was no truth in the tales, as the couple remained as devoted as ever, there *was* one contentious issue about which they could not agree: a choice between the dignity of the dynasty and the happiness of their daughter, Moretta.

Chapter 19 A Mere Branch of a German Princely Family

In the spring of 1879, Prince Alexander ('Sandro') Battenberg – the son of a morganatic marriage between a Hessian prince and a lady-in-waiting – was chosen as the Sovereign Prince of the newly autonomous Bulgaria. His appointment was thanks largely to the support of his uncle, Tsar Alexander II[ii]; and Queen Victoria and Vicky agreed that he was an excellent choice as he was 'sensible', 'clever', 'handsome' and 'manly yet modest.'

Despite his inexperience, Sandro applied himself to his duties and quickly won the support of the Bulgarians but, in 1881, the assassination of his protector and supporter, the Tsar, left him in a precarious position. The new Tsar, Alexander III, despised his Battenberg cousin, and was so infuriated by his refusal to act as a Russian puppet that he sent agents into Bulgaria to stir up unrest. In desperate need of allies, Sandro visited several European courts and, in the summer of 1883, his search took him to Potsdam, where he won the heart of seventeen-year-old Moretta.

While Fritz was away in Spain, Moretta confessed to her mother that she and Sandro hoped to marry; and Vicky told Queen Victoria, who believed it would be a suitable match. Moretta, however, dreaded telling her father as she knew that he would be appalled by the thought of her marrying the son of a lady-in-waiting. Fritz had been shocked when he heard that her cousin, Victoria of Hesse[jj], was betrothed to Sandro's brother; and, when Moretta summoned the courage to tell him that she wished to marry Sandro, he replied bluntly that he found the idea repugnant.

[ii] Sandro's father, Prince Alexander of Hesse, was the brother of Marie of Hesse, who married Tsar Alexander II in 1841.
[jj] The daughter of Vicky's sister, Alice.

The Prussian Royal Fanily viewed the Battenbergs with such disdain that they initially intended to boycott the Hessian wedding until Queen Victoria, disgusted by such 'snobbery' and determined to support her granddaughter, announced that she would be attending. The lovelorn Moretta watched in despair as her cousin, Victoria, exchanged vows with Louis Battenberg while she dared not even mention Sandro's name to her father.

Her spirits lifted a little the following year when Vicky's youngest sister, Beatrice, married another of the Battenberg brothers[kk]. Surely, she thought, if he were deemed worthy of a daughter of Queen Victoria, there was every reason to hope that her father might reconsider his position. Vicky tirelessly pleaded her case, telling Fritz that their daughter's happiness rested in his hands; and, eventually, to prevent an argument, he replied that he liked Sandro personally and, if he were Emperor, he would consent to the marriage rather than seeing his daughter so unhappy.

In reality, Fritz knew that the Emperor would never agree to the match as he had even threatened to banish Vicky and Moretta if they continued to speak of the subject. Even the liberal-minded Empress thought the idea was preposterous, writing to Queen Victoria that Sandro's parentage made him an inappropriate suitor for a granddaughter of the Emperor.

For his own part, much as he wanted to please Vicky and to secure Moretta's happiness, Fritz's 'exalted feeling of dignity and majesty' made him 'opposed to the marriage of a Princess of his House with a scion of a mere branch of a German princely family.'[263] He agreed with his father that a far more appropriate candidate was Prince Carlos, the eldest son of the King of Portugal, but, due to Carlos'

[kk] Prince Henry ('Liko') of Battenberg

Catholicism and Moretta's continued attachment to Sandro, the idea came to nothing.

Bismarck's son, Herbert, who lacked his father's genius but shared his ambition, exacerbated the Battenberg situation by presenting Fritz with a letter from the Charges d'Affairs, Count Wedel, describing how Sandro had bragged of Moretta's declarations of love for him.

'Who's been demanding declarations from my daughter?' Fritz cried. 'What on earth is going on behind my back?'

He raged against all the Battenbergs and even criticised Queen Victoria for allowing her daughter to marry Sandro's brother.

"If I have any say in the matter, I'll take good care that my Battenberg brother-in-law only appears in the court lists as Royal Highness of Great Britain. It is a scandal that the Queen has made him a Royal Highness; it's as if we wanted to do the same for the Marquess of Lorne[ll]."[264]

In spite of his outburst, his critics feared that, sooner or later, he would yield to Vicky's wishes, and so they persuaded the Emperor to secure a promise from his son that he would never consent to a marriage of his daughter and 'the grandson of a valet'.

When Fritz had made that promise, the Emperor asked him if Vicky and Moretta were still pursuing the match; and, although Fritz denied it, the Emperor remarked that he 'did not express himself very clearly. In politics he was ruled by his wife. And, generally, he complained that the Crown Prince was so reserved towards him."[265]

[ll] The Marquis of Lorne had married Queen Victoria's daughter, Louise. Fritz was referring to the fact that Henry Battenberg was a German and, therefore, since Queen Victoria had raised him to the rank of Royal Highness, the Germans might as well give a similar title to Lorne.

Torn between his promise to his father, and Vicky's persistent pleading, Fritz asked Bismarck to prepare a memo detailing all the political arguments against the 'Battenberg alliance'. The most significant argument was the risk that the marriage would pose to Russo-German relations, which the Chancellor had spent several months securing. Privately, Bismarck remarked that he would never jeopardise friendship with Russia to please 'a hysterical female', but in responding to Fritz' request, he set out a more respectful explanation.

"If [Sandro] were accepted as a member of the German Imperial House," he wrote, "it would fill the Emperor [of Russia] with a suspicion which nothing could dissipate. It would be a permanent threat to peace…He would hold it to be a confirmation of all the old doubts as to our sincerity which we had proved to be unfounded, and the Russian press would renew its agitation with the same violence and malice as formerly, and with more success."[266]

Unable to comprehend that Vicky was motivated solely by love for her daughter, Bismarck suspected that she was deliberately trying to create divisions between Germany and Russia, so that the Germans would be driven into an alliance with Britain. It suited him that the Russians had begun a whispering campaign to sully Sandro's reputation with claims that he was homosexual, or that he kept a harem of mistresses and indulged in all kinds of unnatural practices.

"Lord Salisbury," Queen Victoria wrote to her Prime Minister, "cannot be aware of the fearful insults and positive ill-usage that [Sandro] has met with at the hands of Russia and of the Emperor personally, though he is his first Cousin."[267]

For Fritz, the issue became more complex when William stepping into the dispute and criticised his mother for encouraging Moretta to expect a happy outcome. As

Fritz naturally defended Vicky and reprimanded William for his lack of respect, his critics took his loyalty as proof that he would eventually yield to his wife and consent to the marriage.

It was obvious that Moretta's dreams would not be fulfilled in the Emperor's lifetime, as he, who had once sacrificed love for duty, was far too entrenched in family tradition to change his mind. While staying in Ems in the spring of 1885, however, he suffered a series of 'fainting fits'[mm], and it was widely believed that he was dying. Again, there was intense speculation about what sort of monarch his successor would be, and Fritz' anxious opponents attacked him more vitriolically. Ministers accused him of pettiness in clinging to his royal status; and they mocked his disappointment that he was not widely recognised in Berlin. Holstein complained that he displayed a feminine temperament in preferring to be ill-treated than ignored; and Waldersee described him as displaying 'great vehemence over unimportant matters' and imagining that 'due deference is purposely withheld from him.'[268] Others mocked the monotone with which he delivered speeches, and his lack of understanding of complex affairs of state. More disconcertingly, most agreed that Vicky's influence over him increased every year in proportion to the progressive weakening of his character. Their only hope was that, when he ascended the throne, he would retain Bismarck's services, as the Chancellor was the only man who could keep the English woman's influence in check.

Bismarck, following the speculation with interest, was gratified when General von Abedyll told him that the Crown Prince intended to retain the same government on his accession. A few days later, Fritz invited him to the New Palace and asked him directly if he would continue as Chancellor after the death of his father. Pleasantly surprised

---

[mm] Probably transient ischaemic attacks or 'mini-strokes'.

by his 'kindliness of feeling', Bismarck replied that he would do so on two conditions: parliament must not be allowed to run the country; and there must be no foreign interference in German policy. When Fritz had assured him on both counts, Bismarck warned him that it was vital to avoid the 'English influence', and, for the sake of good relations with Russia, to prevent the Battenberg marriage. Fritz silently pursed his lips, leaving Bismarck to conclude, 'the poor devil agrees with me, but he daren't say so.'[269]

In the event, the discussions were premature as the Emperor soon recovered, but, nine months later, while dining with his family, he was 'seized with a kind of paralysis, became confused in his utterances, and finally lost the power of speech.'[270] He was carried to his bed and, by the following morning, he was much improved but for a severe headache and occasional bouts of confusion.

When the danger had passed, Fritz was sent to Munich for the funeral of 'poor, crazy' Ludwig of Bavaria, who had allegedly killed himself and his doctor after being confined on the grounds of insanity.

> "A very picturesque feature," wrote a witness at the funeral, "were the groups of the various religious orders in their old-world dress. The Crown Prince Frederick, who followed the bier with the Archduke Rudolph, carried his baton of field-marshal. The ceremony in the church lost much by the absence of any music from organ or instrument, and the intoning of the bishops and canons without accompaniment sounded harsh. A magnificent catafalque had been erected to receive the coffin, and a shield bore the inscription: "Ludwig von Bayern Pfalzgraf am Rhein.""[271]

There had been little love lost between Fritz and Ludwig, who had never forgiven him for his 'betrayal' after the Franco-Prussian War. Ludwig had pointedly denied him the prestigious Order of St Hubert Ludwig, and was convinced that when he succeeded his father, the individual states would lose their autonomy, as power would be centralised in Prussia. Although the other German rulers dismissed Ludwig's fears as irrational, there was certainly an element of truth in his prediction. Soon after his return from Munich, while dining with Princess Catherine Radziwill, Fritz stated firmly that the German princes should always remember that they were merely 'peers' of the Empire.[nn]

[nn] 'Les princes Allemands devraient toujours se souvenir qu'ils ne sont que les pairs de l'Empire – p-a-i-r-s – vous me comprenez?'The German princes should always remember that they are only the peers of the Empire – p-e-e-r-s - you understand me?'

Chapter 20 – A Very Gentle Knight

In the early autumn of 1886, Fritz and Vicky and their younger daughters escaped from the tensions in Berlin to Portofino on the Italian Riviera, where they stayed in the villa of the Earl of Carnarvon[oo]. Local dignitaries visited them, as did the King and Queen of Italy, with whom they took a carriage ride on a particularly chilly afternoon. Within hours of returning to the villa, Fritz had developed a cold, and, although the symptoms eventually subsided, he remained hoarse throughout the winter.

New Year brought the usual round of balls and social functions, and, as the hoarseness persisted, he was examined by the court physician, Dr Wegner. The usual remedies for sore throats and tonsillitis were of no avail and, in February, he told an English guest at the spectacular Carnival Court Ball, 'I cannot talk to you much, my throat is so bad.'"[272]

On 6th March, following a consultation with Wegner, Professor Gerhardt, a specialist from the University of Berlin, performed a laryngoscopy. Holding a mirror attached to a stick between his teeth, he examined the epiglottis and vocal cords, on one of which he discovered a polyp. Gerhardt recommended an excision, and spent several days preparing Fritz for the procedure by administering cocaine and accustoming his throat to a number of surgical instruments. Painful and irritating as they were, these preliminary operations were but a prelude to a far more unpleasant series of treatments. Gerhardt attempted to remove the polyp with a wire snare but, having succeeded only in scraping a thin white membrane from its surface, he repeated the procedure using a circular

---

[oo] Ironically, in the light of subsequent events, Carnarvon had been suffering from a throat complaint and had received letter from a cousin, warning him that Portofino was not a suitable place for anyone with a throat condition.

knife. As this was equally unproductive, Gerhardt was left with no other option but to cauterise the polyp with an incandescent wire. Cauterisation was repeated at least thirteen times over the subsequent month, with only one week's respite to allow Fritz to participate in his father's ninetieth birthday celebrations.

The cauterisations served only to spread the growth across the larynx, and left Fritz so exhausted and disheartened that he sighed that he knew he was dying. Making no allowance for the effects of cocaine, one attendant reported:

"His moods...altered rapidly and inexplicably. Sometimes he appeared dull, weary, almost sleepy and unwilling to speak or move, glancing aimlessly about him as if thinking of something other than present matters; then suddenly roused to startling gayety...as if he saw it draped in the rosiest hues."[273]

On Wegner's advice, he spent much of April resting in Ems, from where Vicky wrote to her mother that his throat was improving and he was in far better spirits. Sadly, she was deceiving herself, just as her mother had deceived herself a quarter of a century earlier when she refused to accept the seriousness of Prince Albert final illness. Fritz could barely speak when he returned to Berlin on 15th May, and, when Gerhardt re-examined him, he found that the tumour had grown considerably. Fritz asked him to resume the cauterisations but Gerhardt, suspecting that the growth might be cancerous, ominously replied that he would prefer to obtain a second opinion.

Gerhardt sent for a renowned surgeon, Ernest von Bergmann, who had recently left St Petersburg to take up a professorship at the University of Berlin. Bergmann diagnosed an epithelioma[pp] and, although he could not say

---

[pp] An abnormal growth on the epithelium – the tissue that covers the surface of organs.

whether or not it was malignant, he recommended a complete laryngectomy. He did not explain to Fritz the details of the procedure, which involved cutting the throat from the outside and would leave his patient permanently voiceless. Although Bergmann played down the risks, his colleagues were alarmed at the prospect of such a dangerous operation; and, when Bismarck learned what was happening, he hastily intervened.

"The doctors determined," he wrote in his diary, "to make the Crown Prince unconscious and to carry out the removal of the larynx without having informed him of their intentions. I raised objections, and required that they should not proceed without the consent of the Crown Prince. The Emperor, after being informed by me, forbade them to carry out the operation without the consent of his son."[274]

At Bismarck's insistence, a whole posse of doctors – Gerhardt; Wegner; Bergmann; the Emperor's physician, Dr Lauer; Fritz' surgeon, Dr Schrader; and a throat specialist, Professor Tobold from Berlin – gathered to re-examine Fritz' throat and to discuss alternative treatments. This time, unbeknown to Fritz, they all agreed that the growth was probably cancerous and that there was no alternative to a complete laryngectomy.

A date was set for the operation – 21st May – but it required the Emperor's permission, and, when the doctors requested a meeting, he carelessly replied that it was inconvenient as he had arranged to inspect the troops in Potsdam. Even when they impressed upon him the seriousness of the situation, he appeared unconcerned but eventually agreed to see them briefly before leaving for the barracks.

As soon as he had obtained the Emperor's consent, Bergmann began hiring nurses and preparing an operating theatre in the New Palace, but Bismarck, genuinely concerned for Fritz' life, insisted on postponing surgery until they had obtained yet another medical opinion. A list was compiled of all the leading throat specialists from across the continent, one of whom was an English physician, Morell Mackenzie. Mackenzie had the right credentials, as he had written several books on the subject and had been instrumental in the founding of the London Hospital for Diseases of the Throat[qq]. Vicky hesitated before agreeing to his appointment as she feared the repercussion if his treatment were unsuccessful. The German doctors could use him as a scapegoat for their own shortcomings, and she would be accused of having selected an Englishman instead of a German.

Nonetheless, Wegner and Bergmann strongly favoured Mackenzie, and so, on 18th May, Vicky telegrammed her mother asking her to send him to Potsdam without delay. That night, Queen Victoria asked her own doctor, Sir James Reid, to visit him in Harley Street to explain the situation. Mackenzie was on his way to be when Reid arrived, but he promised that he would take the first train to Berlin the following morning.

Although the doctors had not told Fritz that they suspected the growth was cancerous, they warned him that surgery would leave him unable to speak. Fearing that this would prevent him from carrying out his duties as Emperor, he informed his father – without telling Vicky – that he had no desire to reign and, if he survived the operation, he would abdicate in favour of William.

> "This declaration was within a brief space of time repeated in the presence of Prince Bismarck, and was by him reduced to writing. The paper was deposited among the official private archives of the Crown at Berlin."[275]

[qq] Queen Victoria's doctor failed to see the necessity of a hospital devoted solely to throat conditions and joked that soon there would be a hospital for diseases of the big toe!

On the afternoon of 20th May, Mackenzie arrived at the New Palace and, before even being permitted to change his clothes, he was taken to examine the royal patient. After a brief consultation with his German counterparts, he performed a laryngoscopy and observed a pea-like protuberance on the left vocal cord, which accounted for Fritz' hoarse whisper.

Leaving Fritz in the darkened room to await his diagnosis, he told the German doctors that there was no means of knowing if the growth were malignant without a biopsy. To his surprise, none of the Germans felt equipped to carry out such a procedure and so it would be left to Mackenzie to do it. Unfortunately, he had forgotten to bring his own forceps with him, and so he had to rely on unfamiliar instruments.

> "The first introduction of the cup-like blades failed to close upon and secure any fragment of the tumour," he wrote, "but the second attempt, the result of which was greeted with a look of amazement, followed by one of annoyance and disappointment, brought away a bit of the growth."[276]

The extracted tissue was sent to Professor Virchow at the Berlin Institute for Pathology, and, while awaiting the results, Fritz enjoyed a few days' rest from the painful treatments. He could not escape, though, from the anguish of wondering what Virchow might discover or what had caused the illness. While walking in the gardens with Mackenzie, he said that, contrary to popular opinion, he had never been a heavy smoker, although the public thought otherwise because a picture of him holding a pipe had been widely circulated during the Franco-Prussian War. The pipe, he explained, was merely a prop to create the impression that he was perfectly relaxed about the war's progress, but, when he tried to smoke it, it had made him feel ill. Oddly, though, a guest, who visited the New Palace in the mid-1870s, described spending an evening with Fritz and Vicky, during which 'the Prince smoked his long pipe', which the Princess occasionally refilled with tobacco[277].

Mackenzie blithely assured him that he could be cured, and, when Fritz asked him directly if the growth were cancerous, he calmly advised him to wait for the results of the biopsy.

Disappointingly, Virchow reported that the sample he had received was too small to enable him to make a diagnosis, and he asked for the biopsy to be repeated. By 7th June, Mackenzie's forceps had arrived from England, and, much to Gerhard's disgust, he pulled them from his pocket and, without disinfecting them, began the procedure. Mackenzie would later claim that they were kept in a sterile bag within his breast pocket, but Gerhardt was also perturbed by several other aspects of his treatment. The light, which should have illuminated the vocal cords, was positioned in such a way as to light only Fritz's cheek; and, after fishing around for several minutes but failing to obtain a sample, Mackenzie decided to abandon the procedure for that day. When he had gone, Gerhardt examined Fritz' throat and, on discovering that both vocal cords were reddened and sore, he asked Wegner to accompany him to confront Mackenzie in person.

> "I...told him," Gerhardt later wrote, "that he had grasped the until then healthy right vocal band instead of the left one with his strong forceps, and had bruised and torn it."[278]

As a result, Gerhardt claimed, Fritz was unable to speak at all for several weeks and both sides of his throat were more painful.

> "This is perhaps," Gerhardt concluded, "the first well-authenticated case in which a laryngologist, through carelessness, endeavoured to tear a piece out of a healthy vocal band."[279]

Although Mackenzie's third attempt at the biopsy was more successful, the German doctors' criticism had had sparked a dispute that became more acrimonious with every treatment. Mackenzie, who revelled in publicity, told the press that the German doctors were more concerned about their own reputations than the well-being of the Crown Prince, who would have been better served if he had 'presented himself as an ordinary patient at the Throat Hospital and been treated incognito.'[280] Soon stories appeared in German and British newspapers, accusing Bergmann and his colleagues of having misdiagnosed cancer, and claiming that only Mackenzie's timely intervention had saved the Crown Prince from an unnecessary and dangerous laryngotomy. Bergmann, incensed that Mackenzie had been leaking false information, later insisted that:

> "Not a word was spoken in May 1887 regarding any other operation than the opening of the larynx as a means of extirpating the small growth that was at the left portion of the vocal band. This, in fact, was the only growth under consideration at the time. I desire to emphasize this fact, as the press, which attacked us, has been constantly pleased to speak of total extirpation of the larynx."[281]

While the doctors squabbled, further quarrels erupted in Fritz' household when a rumour spread that William and Bismarck had found an ancient law that forbade a man who could not speak from becoming king. Although there was no truth whatsoever in the tale, it further convinced Vicky that William was trying to usurp his father; and when she heard a rumour that Fritz had offered to abdicate, she believed that William had invented the story to further his own ambition.

Fritz was more put out when William volunteered to replace him as the Emperor's representative at the at the forthcoming celebrations for Queen Victoria's Golden

Jubilee. In fact, although William would have relished playing a prominent role in the celebrations, he was acting on the advice of the German doctors, who warned him that the journey would be too tiring for his father. The ever-optimistic Mackenzie, however, announced that the tumour had not grown since his first examination and, when Virchow reported that that the growth was a warty thickening of the larynx ('pachydermia verrucose largyngis') and he had found no evidence of cancer, he assured Fritz that there was no reason why he should not go to England.

The German doctors were sceptical, as pachydermia was usually associated with alcoholism, and it rarely affected only one vocal cord. Convinced that Mackenzie wanted Fritz to go to England so that he could take sole charge of his treatment, they derided his recommendation of a stay on the Isle of Wight so the sea air could aid his recuperation, and asked Bismarck to persuade the Emperor to prevent his son from leaving. Ironically, the Emperor who had so often treated Fritz as a child, replied that he was a grown man and could make his own decisions.

By then, though, Vicky was making virtually all of the decisions about Fritz' treatment, and she clung to Mackenzie's optimistic prognosis that the illness could be cured. Privately, Fritz was less convinced by the Englishman's almost flippant buoyancy, and he knew that Virchow had not ruled out cancer but had merely found no evidence of it in the small sample that he had tested. Nonetheless, he was eager to take part in the jubilee celebrations and insisted that he was well enough for the journey. Gerhardt then pleaded that he and his colleagues should be allowed to accompany him but, unwilling to arrive in England with an army of doctors, Fritz replied that he was placing himself entirely in Mackenzie's care. As a concession, he agreed to be accompanied by Wegner and Dr Landgraf, who was skilled at performing laryngoscopies, on the understanding that they could examine his throat but were to take no active part in his treatment.

Chapter 21 – An Ideal Prince Among Princes

Amid huge displays of bright summer flowers and a myriad of flags fluttering on roof tops and railings, crowds poured in to London from all across the country, eager to catch a glimpse of the greatest procession of royalty that the city had ever seen. So many princes and princesses were crammed into the royal palaces that some of Vicky's nieces had to share a bed, and equerries slept in alcoves or on the straw in the stables.

Anticipating the crowds, Vicky had had the foresight to lease a comfortable house in the suburbs of Upper Norwood, where Fritz could recuperate from the long journey away from the bustle of central London. Even in Norwood, though, he could not escape the squabbling doctors when Landgraf observed that his throat was inflamed but Mackenzie firmly denied it. Deeply troubled, Landgraf asked Fritz to ensure that Wegner was informed if Mackenzie made any changes to his treatment, but, 'This proposal was very promptly rejected.'[282]

Nor was there any respite from the tortuous treatments, as Mackenzie was administering perchloride of iron – a solution frequently used for diseases of the throat as well as venereal disease and ulcerating cancers – which created such a painful burning sensation that it was necessary to apply ice immediately after each application.

On the evening of 20th June, six days after he arrived in England, he and Vicky met the rest of the guests at a stately banquet in Buckingham Palace. The next day was the main event of the celebrations: a procession from the palace to Westminster Abbey for a Thanksgiving Service. Shortly after eleven o'clock, the Queen's daughters and granddaughters set out in a series of carriages, followed by a pageant of mounted kings and princes, including the Kings of Denmark, Greece and Saxony; and the Princes of Portugal, Austria and Sweden.

Even in such illustrious company, Fritz stood out above the rest, in his brilliant white uniform, silver breast-plate and the imperial-eagle crested helmet of the Cuirassier Guards. 'A towering Lohengrin-like figure,' according to several witnesses; 'outwardly the embodiment of princely grace and splendour;'[283] he rode 'with the firm easy seat of a cavalry soldier, holding the baton of a German Field-Marshal: an ideal prince among princes."[284]

Although one or two people in the crowd noticed that he looked 'pale and grey', few suspected that he was seriously ill. Two days later, however, an article appeared in the press, claiming that an anonymous Viennese doctor had asserted that the Crown Prince had a terminal illness. The unnamed doctor admitted that he had not examined the patient but he remarked that a simple polyp could have been removed in a matter of minutes and the Crown Prince would recovered in under a fortnight. The secrecy surrounding his condition was due to its severity and the surgeons' failure to perform a complete laryngectomy, which was the only means of securing his survival. Now, said the doctor ominously, any malignant growth would have spread, and the physicians could only 'ameliorate the condition of the patient until the inevitable termination occurs.' Others newspapers took up the story, with a variety of speculative reports, prompting numerous quacks to publish books and treatises, recommending 'efficacious' treatments, ranging from electrical impulses to the avoidance of all fluids.

Kept largely ignorant of the speculation, Fritz went daily to Mackenzie's Harley Street home; and, on July 15th, he visited the London Hospital for Diseases of the Throat, where he was happy to chat with several of the patients.

> "A little girl who had undergone the operation of tracheotomy was sitting up in bed nursing a doll. On being asked by the Crown Prince, 'Which is the patient, you or the doll?' the little mite answered,

'Sure I don't know which it is, my dear!' which delighted His Imperial Highness."[285]

A few days later, he left London for Norris Castle on the Isle of Wight, which he and Vicky had leased for the summer. By then, the exertion of making so many polite conversations had left him barely able to speak but, strolling among the peacocks on the lawns, and inhaling the fresh sea breeze that drifted across the Solent, he was more optimistic about the possibility of a full recovery. When he chanced to meet Vicky's nieces on the beach, he became positively playful.

"He could not talk to us," wrote one of the nieces, "but I remember how he pretended to bombard us with sand and dry seaweed. He was jolly and yet one somehow felt he was condescending, which made us feel shy."[286]

In early August, he and Vicky moved north to Braemar in the Scottish Highlands, accompanied by Mark Hovell, a surgeon from the Hospital for Diseases of the Throat. At Braemar, as at Balmoral, he had the freedom to wander among the local people, and a touching scene occurred when a boatman man asked him to name a new steam launch. Without a second's hesitation, he glanced at Vicky and pronounced, 'The White Heather', recalling the moment over a quarter of a century earlier, when he had handed her a sprig of white heather as a sign of his love.

As Wegner and Landgraf were staying over ninety miles away in Edinburgh, Fritz enjoyed not having to listen to the doctors' endless quarrels, but he could not help overhearing the mutterings of his attendants, who shivered in the bitter winds, complaining that so bleak a climate was hardly suitable for a man with a serious illness. Nonetheless, when Mackenzie arrived a few days later, he blithely told Queen Victoria that Fritz' throat had 'never looked so well' and, with time and patience, he would fully recover. Delighted by the news, the Queen, at Fritz' request, knighted Mackenzie in the Drawing Room of Balmoral Castle.

Queen Victoria's personal physician, James Reid, was unimpressed by Mackenzie's insouciant optimism and blatant self-promotion but, when he raised the matter with Queen, she refused to listen. When Fritz decided that he should briefly return to Germany, the Queen went further and advised him to ignore those 'two useless doctors who will counteract all Mackenzie's treatment.'[287]

In fact, Mackenzie had begun to doubt his own diagnosis, and privately warned Vicky that, although the growth did not *appear* to be malignant, there was a possibility that 'the disease might be cancerous already, or cancer might develop later on.'[288] Vicky, unwilling to depress Fritz, did not mention Mackenzie's warning; and Mackenzie himself admitted that:

> "With the Crown Prince, I of course could not discuss the situation with the same freedom; but whilst encouraging him as to his condition, I was careful not to say anything of a misleading character."[289]

On returning to Germany, Fritz heeded Queen Victoria's advice and told Bergmann and Gerhardt that, in view of Mackenzie's favourable prognosis, there was no need for them to carry out a further examination.

Vicky was convinced that mountain air was most conducive to Fritz' recovery and so, after a brief stay in Munich, they set out with their younger daughters for the Austrian Tyrol. To distract herself from Mackenzie's worrying warnings, she took long walks and painted the stunning scenery until late September as the weather grew colder and the family moved to the Hotel de Europe in Venice. From there, Vicky wrote to a friend that Fritz was 'unable to be out much, and may not speak, though, alas! He will not obey the strict injunctions of the doctor, and refrain from using his voice more than a very little! It is very difficult in a town, and going about, which, of course, amuses and interests him.'[290] As the town was too crowded, they soon moved on to Baveno, where they stayed in the Villa Clara, a relatively new gothic mansion, built and owned by a Scottish railway contractor, Sir Charles Henfrey[rr].

Relaxing on the shores of Lake Maggiore, Fritz enjoyed an unexpectedly cordial visit from his sons, William and Henry, but even as they relaxed in such an idyllic setting, they could not escape from the constant criticism from Berlin. Fritz was 'dreadfully annoyed' to read complaints in the German press that Vicky had employed an English rather than a German doctor; and that they had opted to stay in the home of a Briton in Italy, rather than in the home of German. There were hints, too, that, as perchloride of iron was used to treat venereal disease, Fritz must have contracted syphilis during his visit to Egypt, eighteen years earlier. The Foreign Minister wrote to Vicky, telling her bluntly that the Berliners blamed her for preventing the Crown Prince's return, but she replied equally brusquely that she was tired of being the scapegoat, 'picked to pieces by people who have no right and no business to meddle in our affairs.'[291]

As Vicky became increasingly stressed, tensions mounted within the household, where what she described as a 'subterranean war' was raging. Fritz' attendants complained that she had ignored warnings that the Tyrolean climate was not conducive to his recovery, and asked why she was dragging a sick man all over the continent when he would have been far more comfortable resting in Berlin or Potsdam.

"I cannot tell you how that woman gets on my nerves," wrote one member of the suite. "During our walks she runs ahead like a mad thing until the

---

[rr] The villa is now known as Villa Henfrey-Branca

Crown Prince comes to a standstill, exhausted, and says: 'I can't go any further. My wife is racing ahead again.' I stay with [him] then, but the Princess just walks on, saying with a soft upward glance: 'You will walk really slowly, won't you, dear Fritz, so that you don't get too hot?'...I cannot bear to see that everlasting smile on her face. The woman has driven every good genius out of her house with that smile."[292]

Struggling to come to terms with the thought that her beloved husband might be dying, Vicky tried to maintain at least a semblance of normality but this, too, prompted deeper resentment. Ignoring suggestions from members of the household, she refused to change the customary lunch time and, consequently, on hot days, the Crown Prince was forced to sit out in the heat of the midday sun.

More disturbingly, a malicious rumour spread that she was having an affair with the comptroller, Count Gotz Burkhard Seckendorff, while her English doctor was slowly poisoning her husband. Her lady-in-waiting, Countess Perponcher, was said to have been utterly astonished when she realised that 'a particularly warm understanding' existed between the Crown Princess and Seckendorff as together they walked up a mountain and spent an excessively long time alone. When they returned, the Countess said, Fritz' obvious delight at seeing her was 'equalled only by her indifference.'[293]

The insinuations were entirely unjustified, as Vicky's interest in Seckendorff went no deeper than their shared knowledge and appreciation of art[ss]. Moreover, when there were so few people whom she and Fritz could trust, he proved himself to be a 'most loyal and devoted friend to his royal master and mistress in the days when

---

[ss] Seckendorff was also a gifted watercolourist.

friends were few, and through all the stormy vicissitudes...when his position was a very difficult one, he showed a wise and brave discretion.'[294] In fact, though, Vicky was often exasperated by his behaviour, and she considered him 'vain' and a *'faiseur d'embarras'*[tt][295]. Several of her acquaintances went further, believing that Bismarck had appointed him 'to restrain the Crown Princess', by choosing her friends and deciding whom she could meet.

For his part, Seckendorff was not always as discreet or as devoted as Vicky and Fritz believed; and, while visiting England, he spent a whole hour pointing out Vicky's shortcomings to Lady Mary Ponsonby.

> "He said he need not explain to me what her qualities were, but that her imprudences were much to be regretted because they led her into such indirect paths, so that Bismarck for one was always on the look-out and thought she was intriguing when she wasn't...I think she is less under S.'s thumb than [people believe]. She certainly snubbed him the day she was here."[296]

Nonetheless the slanderous stories of the affair were widely believed, and Fritz' attendants repeatedly urged him to return home for the sake of his position and reputation. When Vicky was absent, he appeared to agree, but when she returned, he instantly altered his opinion, and so, rather than going home when the time came to leave Baveno, they migrated to San Remo on the Italian Riviera. There, they leased the 'very expensive' Villa Zirio, a stunning white mansion with spacious gardens and nurseries, owned by an Italian lawyer. The people of the region were so delighted to welcome them that they decided to name a new promenade *Corso Frederico*, in Fritz' honour.

[tt] Pretentious.

On 4th November, Hovell arrived in San Remo, and was alarmed to see how substantially the tumour had grown. He immediately sent for Mackenzie, who arrived the following evening; and, on the morning of 6th November, Fritz was examined in the presence of all the doctors. This time even Mackenzie was forced to acknowledge the devastating diagnosis.

"I informed His Imperial Highness that a very unfavourable change had taken place in his throat. He said 'Is it cancer?'' to which I replied, 'I am sorry to say, Sir, it looks very much like it, but it is impossible to be certain…The Crown Prince received the communication with perfect calmness. After a moment of silence, he grasped my hand and said, with that smile of peculiar sweetness, which so well expressed the mingled gentleness and strength of his character, 'I have lately been fearing something of this sort'…In all my long experience I have never seen a man bear himself under similar circumstances with such unaffected heroism."[297]

After months of fluctuating between hope and despair, it was almost a relief for Fritz to know that the suspense was over. He left the room with no show of emotion and continued his usual routine as though nothing untoward had happened. The tension of suspense faded, and, as his voice became clearer, he cheerfully remarked that he had never felt better. He felt so well that he was able to undergo a dental operation, and he calmly discussed the palliative measures that the doctors recommended. Saccharine was removed from his diet, as it was believed to accelerate the growth of tumours; and he was encouraged to take daily carriage rides as the fresh air would be beneficial.

Meanwhile, in Berlin, when initial vague reports reached the Emperor, he was anxious to know more details of the prognosis. He asked his grandson, William, to accompany a trusted physician, Dr Schmidt, to San Remo to obtain a full account from the Crown Prince's doctors and report their findings directly to him.

For Vicky, stressed, exhausted, slandered, and desperately clinging to the hope that Fritz would somehow recover, William's arrival in San Remo ignited all the emotions that she had suppressed for so long. Without allowing him to speak, she exploded in a bitter tirade, accusing him of having come to steal the crown from his father. 'She treated me like a dog,'[298] William gasped; and, when Vicky's anger had subsided, she confessed to her mother that she was ashamed to have 'pitched into him with…considerable violence.'[299] To make matters worse, she saw that Fritz had overheard every word she had said.

As her rage cooled, William arranged the meeting with the doctors, and was 'filled with grief and sorrow'[300] when they explained that Fritz' illness was incurable. Before returning to Berlin with the tragic news, he told his mother of the persistent rumours circulating in the capital and suggested that it would be better if she were to dismiss Mackenzie and rely instead solely on German doctors. This served only to re-ignite her fury, which intensified when newspapers claimed that William had left San Remo with a signed copy of his father's abdication. Wrongly assuming that William was behind the reports, she responded by denying him any further access to his father, and complaining to Queen Victoria of his cruel and unfilial behaviour.

By then, though, Queen Victoria realised that anxiety was clouding Vicky's judgement, and she began to suspect that Mackenzie was neither as skilled nor as reliable as she had initially believed. Several British doctors, including James Reid, expressed serious doubts about Mackenzie's discernment, and they believed that, by refusing to recommend a laryngectomy, he was denying the Crown Prince any hope of survival. Even if, some argued, the tumour were not malignant, its continued growth could eventually lead to asphyxiation. Queen Victoria gradually accepted their explanation, writing in her journal that:

"It must be born in mind that palliatives cannot eradicate the disease, whereas the operation of opening the throat and removing all the growths might do so."[301]

It troubled her, too, that Mackenzie's reports frequently appeared in the press, leaving her in no doubt that he was supplying journalists with confidential information. So great was her concern that she ordered a message to be included in the Court Circular, stating that the majority of reports were speculative and unfounded.

'Some people also think,' she wrote to Vicky, 'that Sir M. Mackenzie's judgement is not quite equal to his great skill in the internal operation'[302]; and, when Vicky's friend, Lady Mary Ponsonby, visited San Remo, she also advised her that, 'with the existing jealousy on the part of the German doctors it may not be wise to call in the English doctor alone.'[303] No one, though – not even Queen Victoria – could persuade Vicky to abandon the only doctor who, through his contradictory reports, gave her hope that Fritz might yet recover.

Queen Victoria also looked carefully into the allegations that Bismarck and William were trying to remove Fritz from the line of succession. Following an interview with the German Ambassador, Count Hatzfeldt, she was able to assure Vicky and Fritz that there was no truth in the rumour as neither Bismarck nor William had any desire to replace him. Soon afterwards, this was substantiated by a message from the Reichstag, assuring him of the Empire's sympathy and loyalty; and, as Christmas approached, gifts and messages of support from public bodies and hundreds of individual well-wishers poured into San Remo.

Mackenzie added to the winter cheer when he decided that the illness *might* not be cancer. In a report, which he sent to the Emperor and published in several medical magazines, he reiterated that there was no evidence of malignancy but solely of chronic laryngitis. Buoyed by Queen Victoria's assurances and Mackenzie's groundless optimism, Fritz became far less 'fidgety' and, when Mary Ponsonby joined his family and guests for dinner, she observed that he 'looked beautiful, with a fresh colour and a good appetite and whom I had the greatest difficulty to prevent talking.'[304]

Charlotte and Henry arrived for Christmas in San Remo, where the usual customs were happily observed, with gifts laid out on tables for the family and members of the household; and on New Year's Eve, Moretta and Henry performed an amusing 'piece' for their parents' entertainment.

Chapter 22 – To Suffer Without Complaint

The new year, 1888, did not begin well. In January, Fritz' became aware of an article, published the previous month in *The Ecclesiastic Review*:
> "Let us pray every day and every hour for our Royal Family, and in particular for the old man [i.e. the Emperor] and for the young man [i.e. William] of this race of heroes. May God in his mercy grant that the terrible punishment which has overtaken the sick Prince Frederick bear fruit, and may it bring resignation to his mind and peace to his conscience."[305]

It soon came to light that the author, Pastor Stoecker, had also been telling his congregation that Germany would enjoy a glorious future when the Emperor died and the throne passed to his grandson.

The insult could not have come at a more inopportune moment. In the first week of the year, Mark Hovell discovered a new growth on Fritz' right vocal cord; and a repulsive odour, coming from his mouth, filled the entire room. On 16th January, struggling to breathe, he developed a severe headache with a high temperature; and the following morning, he coughed up a lump of tissue, which Virchow analysed and found to be a decomposing piece of his larynx.

In the days that followed, it became clear that the growth was gradually blocking his windpipe and sooner rather than later, a tracheotomy would be required. Fritz received this news with his customary equanimity; and Bergmann's assistant, Dr Bramann was hastily installed in San Remo to carry out the procedure at a moment's notice. In early February, Mackenzie was so concerned that he asked Bramann to prepare for the operation but Bramann, put out that he had only been allowed limited access to the patient, insisted on summoning Bergmann and awaiting his arrival. Bergmann was still two days away when, on the night of 8th February, Fritz began gasping for breath so desperately that Mackenzie declared that he would die if Bramann failed to performed the tracheotomy the following morning.

"I am again very anxious and much tormented because tracheotomy is pending," Vicky wrote to a friend, "and you can imagine how I hate the thought of this detestable operation, but if the difficulty of breathing continues and even increases, what else can be done? It makes me miserable, however, that my poor darling should have all this to go through without one's being able to take it away from him, which I gladly would."[306]

The following morning, the anxious doctors fell into another dispute when Mackenzie discovered that Bramann intended to anaesthetise Fritz with chloroform. It was far too dangerous for such an operation, Mackenzie argued, adding that it was never used in England. Bramann curtly replied that it was standard practice in Germany and he had carried out over four hundred tracheotomies without encountering any problems. When Mackenzie continued to protest, Bramann exasperatedly warned that he would not perform the tracheotomy without it; and Mackenzie finally yielded but not before writing a note renouncing all responsibility for the procedure and its outcome.

When sedation had been administered, Bramann nervously cut into the windpipe, and suddenly Fritz' pulse grew weak and the colour drained from his face. For a moment, it appeared that he was dying but Bramann continued the procedure and, when it was complete, his patient woke up and vomited. Within minutes, he came fully to his senses and, with an expression of relief, signalled that he felt much better now that he could breathe.

Vicky had been waiting in an adjoining room with Henry and her daughters, and they embraced one another in joyful relief that the operation had been successful. For a couple of day, the tension in the household eased until Bergmann arrived and insisted that he and his colleagues should take full responsibility for Fritz' future treatment. Vicky resented his presence and the brusqueness of his manner, and was appalled when he roughly introduced a larger canula, causing Fritz intense discomfort and making the wound bleed. A sample of the blood was taken for analysis and, as Virchow was unavailable, it was sent to a Professor Waldeger, who discovered evidence of cancer.

Vicky stubbornly refused to believe Waldeger's findings. 'You will have heard,' she wrote to Queen Victoria, 'that this Prof. Waldeger of Berlin…says he found undoubted evidence of cancer…This quite convinces Bergmann, Bramann etc. I own it fails quite to convince me.'[307]

A few days later, she wrote in a similar vein to a friend:

> "They base all on their newest microscopic examinations – to which we are to trust, seeing that what Virchow so explicitly said so short a time ago in no way corresponds with what Waldeger now says. I am more troubled and distressed than I can say – quite miserable sometimes, and yet I cannot bring myself to see things irrevocably in the very worst light, there are so many ifs and buts. I think my dear husband's general condition much improved these last few days; though that odious bleeding goes on, and the nights are much broken. His appetite is really improving and he looks much better."[308]

Unaware of the results of the blood test, Fritz recuperated quietly in his rooms, reading and finding inspiration in Thomas a Kempis' *The Imitation of Christ.*

Meanwhile, in Berlin, the Emperor had caught a chill and, as he feared his health was deteriorating, he began to consider the possibility of requiring a regency. As Fritz was ill and far away, he appointed William as *Stellvertreter des Kaisers* (Vice-Emperor), giving him complete authority to act on his behalf, including the right to sign declarations, 'By Order of the King.'

Of course, Fritz would need to be told, but William, knowing that his mother would refuse to allow him to see him, sent his brother, Henry, instead. On hearing of the Emperor's decision, Vicky was so distraught that she complained that Henry had behaved very badly and left Fritz 'much upset, very angry, and much excited.'[309] Deeply offended, too, Fritz wrote to his father to say that, in spite of his physical condition, he was mentally alert and perfectly capable of reading documents and issuing orders.

The Emperor, though, was rapidly fading, and, in early March, Fritz received a number of desperate letters urging him to return to Berlin. His supporters feared that, if the Emperor died and he were still absent, Bismarck would arrange to place William on the throne.

Mackenzie and Vicky agreed that Fritz was not well enough to travel, and, on 7th March, Vicky told a friend, 'Heaven grant that we need not be whisked off to Germany where it is terribly cold now!'[310] That afternoon, Fritz decided that he could delay no longer as he needed to say goodbye to his dying father.

Two days later, preparations were almost complete for his departure from San Remo, and Fritz was taking the air in the gardens when a telegram arrived, addressed to 'His Majesty, the German Emperor Frederick William.'

He burst into tears as this could only mean that his father was dead, and now he faced the daunting prospect of assuming responsibility for the Empire while he was still so weak. That evening, though, he donned his military uniform to perform his first act as Emperor: awarding Vicky the prestigious Order of the Black Eagle.

The journey back to Berlin might have been a personal *Via Dolorosa* for Fritz, who, while grieving for his father, knew that his own reign would be very brief. Although aware that each passing mile was taking him closer to the grave, he remained determinedly cheerful, taking an interest in the changing scenery and acknowledging the crowds who had gathered to applaud him at every station. To prevent further arguments, he made use of the journey to compose a series of instructions for his doctors. Mackenzie was to continue in overall charge of his treatment, while Wegner and an assistant, Krause, were to attend him twice a day, and Bergmann once a week. At ten o'clock, he retired to his compartment and slept quite comfortably until early the following morning as the train approached Munich. At eight o'clock, the Dowager Queen of Bavaria – mother of the ill-fated Ludwig II – joined him and Vicky for breakfast, before they set out for Leipzig, where Bismarck would be waiting to accompany him to the capital.

Standing alongside the Chancellor on the platform in Leipzig Station was the Minister of Justice, Friedberg, whom Fritz had appointed while serving as his father's regent. Since then, Friedberg had received little recognition for his services, but, as he was now in a position to rectify that oversight, Fritz removed his own Order of the Black Eagle and placed it over the minister's shoulders.

Shocked by Fritz' ill and exhausted appearance, and knowing that Berlin would be crowded with guests for the late Emperor's funeral, Bismarck was afraid that the exertion might prove too much for him. Once on the train, he invited Mackenzie to work with him to draw up a suitable timetable to ensure to ensure that the new Emperor was not overtaxed and could rest as often as possible.

At eleven o'clock that night the train finally reached its destination, and William stood on the platform, waiting to greet his father. Fritz acknowledged him graciously but when he moved to greet his mother, she turned her back on him and ignored him completely.

A blizzard was blowing as the imperial carriage made its way to the magnificent seventeenth-century Charlottenburg Palace.

"The intense whiteness of the streets and houses," Mackenzie recorded, "the brilliant illuminations, and the enthusiastic crowds of people, made a very striking picture, and as we drove up to the Castle gates, the Garde du Corps, with their eagle-crested helmets, glittering cuirasses and drawn swords, added to the imposing nature of the scene. His Majesty alighted from his carriage with a firm step, and in passing through the hall, spoke to the British Ambassador and several high officials who were there. He very soon retired to his room, where I followed him and found him rather fatigued by the journey. The shaking of the railway, carriage had slightly increased the discharge from the canula, but on the whole he had borne the excitement remarkably well."[311]

The next morning, his mother arrived, and Fritz hurried down the stairs to greet her. She had not seen him in over a year and was so distressed to see him so grey and breathless that, as they silently embraced one another, they both burst into tears.

On 15th March, as Mackenzie was changing the tracheotomy dressing, a large piece of tissue came away from the wound. To his horror, he realised it was a part of Fritz' windpipe, which was damaged when Bergmann roughly inserted the canula that was too big and too heavy for the aperture. Again, Fritz bore his sufferings with resignation but, the next morning, he could hardly restrain his emotions when Mackenzie reluctantly told him that he was not well enough to attend his father's funeral. More depressed than ever, he shuffled restlessly as the cortege passed his window, repeatedly murmuring, 'I ought to be there.'

His spirits raised a little that afternoon when Mackenzie fitted a new and more comfortable canula; and by the following day he felt well enough to hold meetings with his ministers and other dignitaries from across the Empire.

Fritz knew he had neither the time nor the strength to enact any major reforms, and he was also acutely aware that the country needed Bismarck more than ever. He could not risk his resignation if he pushed him too far, but there were two issues about which he was prepared to confront him. It was customary at the start of a new reign for the King to release political prisoners, and, despite Bismarck's warning that this would give rise to waves of sedition, Fritz insisted on adhering to the tradition. He demanded, too, the removal of the reactionary Minister of the Interior, Robert von Puttkamer, who had been responsible for many of the anti-Catholic laws as well as imposing other draconian measures including prohibiting strikes and public meetings. Fritz also had a more personal reason to wish to be rid of him, as he had publicly criticised him on several occasions and, when he made the official announcement of the late Emperor's death, he deliberately omitted to mention the customary support for his successor.

Fritz also used what time he had to prepare his son for his future role as Emperor. From early April, he gave William a series of duties, and, as he performed them well, he gradually entrusted him with more responsibilities. This went some way to restoring their former relationship.

"Learn to suffer without complaint," Fritz told him on 20th April, and it was a maxim that remained with him for the rest of his life[uu].

[uu] Many years later, long after Williams accession, a joke was frequently heard in Berlin, which contained the line: "What is the Emperor's favourite saying? Suffer without complaint."

Chapter 23 – Sad Reflections

Sitting in the idyllic gardens of the Florentine Villa Palmieri, Queen Victoria was engaged in a battle of wills with her Prime Minister, Lord Salisbury. She had received a poignant letter from Vicky, and, desperate to support her daughter and son-in-law at such a difficult time, she had decided to cut short her holiday and make a detour to Berlin.

Salisbury was aghast, convinced that the visit would seriously damage Anglo-German relations. He had received so many reports from diplomats, military attachés and the British ambassador, warning him that Vicky's outspoken devotion to England had led to many German politicians to believe that she was working in conjunction with the British Government. The ambassador, Edward Malet, had told him of a rumour that she intended to use Fritz' illness as an excuse to rule in his stead, and to impose a British-style constitution on the German Empire. Even her friend, the diplomat, Robert Morier, reported that 'her constant praise of England is the cause of the Court irritation against us'[312]; and Colonel Swaine, the British military attaché in Berlin, stated that the 'honest and excellent' Crown Prince William was, like most of his countrymen, 'aggravated by his mother's English praises.'[313]

Equally disconcerting for Salisbury was the realisation that the Queen would be accompanied by her daughter and son-in-law, Henry Battenberg, which would convince Bismarck conviction that she intended to persuade Fritz to sanction the marriage of Moretta and Sandro. Already the Chancellor had published several derogatory articles about her in the German press; and, if she appeared in Berlin, he would 'vent his fury' upon her.

> "He shows temper against Your Majesty and as at such times he is quite unscrupulous, he will probably try to give currency to statements which

are designed to make Your Majesty personally responsible for any evil results of his own violent passion."[314]

The Queen indignantly replied that she would not yield to Bismarck's 'tyranny'; and she no intention of pressing for the Battenberg match. In fact, she had written to Vicky, advising her to persuade Moretta to abandon hope of ever marrying Sandro, as she was aware that his ardour for the princess had already cooled.

Salisbury adopted a different approach, suggesting that it would be awkward if she were to meet her grandson, William, who would soon become Emperor and was known to be at odds with his mother.

"If any thorny subject came up in conversation," Salisbury warned, "...the Prince might say something that would not reflect credit on him, and that if he acted so as to draw any reproof from your Majesty, he might take it ill, and a feeling would rankle in his mind which might hinder the good relations between the two nations."[315]

The Queen was so affronted that Salisbury dared to interfere in her family affairs that she left his letter unanswered; but she let it be known that, with or without the Prime Minister's support, she would not be dissuaded from visiting her 'poor dying son-in-law.'

Early in the morning of 24th April, she arrived at the small Charlottenburg station, where Vicky, looking pale and thinner, was waiting with her family on the platform. As she rode in an open carriage with her daughter and grandson, the crowds cheered and welcomed her with warmth and affection.

Fritz was desperately disappointed at not being able to get up to greet her, but he was touched when she came to sit by his bedside. Both were deeply moved by the sad circumstances of the visit, but his spirits lifted when, at his request, she described her sojourn in Florence.

Bismarck, much to the delight of the journalists who anticipated a sensational story, requested a meeting with the Queen. While Salisbury sat in London, wringing his hands in fear, the Queen's equerries were amused and astonished to see the Iron Chancellor almost shaking with nerves before being led in to see her. The Queen, too, was 'agreeably surprised' to find him so 'amiable and gentle', and was gratified when he assured her that, even if Fritz were too ill to reign, he would not suggest a regency as that would be hurtful to the Emperor. Clearly, since his accession, Fritz' and Bismarck's relationship had become more harmonious, as Bismarck himself later wrote:

> "At the time of his government I was always on the best of terms with the Emperor Frederick and his consort, the Empress Victoria. Any differences of opinion between us were discussed with Their Majesties in the most friendly way. The Empress Victoria is, moreover, very clever and decided. When I appeared with some business for her imperial consort, she frequently entered the sick-room before me to prepare him and gain him over for my project."[316]

Bismarck assured Queen Victoria that much of the reported rancour between their countries was an invention of the press; and he was relieved to hear that she had no intention of encouraging the Battenberg marriage. When the meeting was over, he left the room, wiping the sweat from his brow and gasping with genuine admiration, 'What a woman! One could do business with her!'

The Queen also arranged a private meeting with Mackenzie, who told her that Vicky was entirely 'alone' and 'betrayed' by intriguers. Although naturally disturbed by what she had heard, the Queen also listened to the advice of the members of her own suite. Her physician, Reid, suggested that Mackenzie was insincere and motivated by self-interest; and her Private Secretary, Henry

Ponsonby, asked, 'Why should the Empress [i.e. Vicky] alone be right [about Mackenzie] and all the rest here wrong?'[317]

Anxious to obtain a fuller picture of the whole situation, the Queen arranged to speak with William and Henry, to hear their side of the argument. Having heard all they had to say, she concluded that there were faults on both sides, and, after advising William to show more respect to his mother, she gently explained to Vicky that, although her son was surrounded by intriguers, she, too, was being misled by her advisors. Although Vicky did not reply, within days of the Queen's departure, Fritz entrusted William with further responsibilities.

When the Queen had left, Fritz told Mackenzie that her visit had done him much good. A few days later, he was well enough to leave his bedroom; and, within a fortnight, he delighted the public by taking short carriage rides through the park.

Although he had missed his father's funeral, there was one happier event that he was determined to attend: the wedding of Henry and Princess Irene of Hesse[vv]. On the eve of the nuptials, he hoped to wait up to welcome Irene to the city, but Mackenzie, fearing he would be too exhausted, persuaded him to retire early to save his strength for the wedding day.

The 24th May began with a civil ceremony in the Blue Gallery of the Charlottenburg, and Fritz rose early in readiness to witness the couple signing the marriage contract. Much to his chagrin, though, it took so long to assist him into his uniform and to tend his tracheotomy that, by the time he reached the gallery, his family had assumed that he would not be coming, and the civil ceremony was already completed. He joined the guests in the chapel for the religious service and, as the breath

---

[vv] Irene was a daughter of Vicky's late sister, Alice.

whistling through his canula sounded above the prayers, all who were present were filled with admiration for his resignation and courage.

Simply sitting through the service had left him so exhausted that he was unable to eat lunch or to participate in the afternoon's celebrations. In the evening, though, he had revived sufficiently to enjoy a carriage ride; and two days later he drove out again with his brother-in-law, the Prince of Wales.

On 29th May, he was delighted when William arranged for him to inspect three regiments under his command. Dressed in full uniform complete with his Orders and medals, he sat in an open carriage to salute the divisions.

> "Whether from the weight of his helmet or from excitement," Mackenzie wrote, "the Emperor's head was bathed in perspiration although the day was not at all hot. Immediately after the inspection I got him some wine, which seemed to revive him. I said to His Majesty, 'I am afraid, Sir, it was rather tiring for you seeing the troops march past.' He replied, 'No, but it is the first time I have seen my soldiers.' The Emperor seemed thoughtful for the rest of the day, and indeed, under the circumstances, there was sufficient matter for sad reflections."[318]

His sad reflections continued the next day when he visited the family mausoleum, undoubtedly thinking that soon he, too, would lie beneath the cold marble. He decided that, in what little time remained to him, he would resolve an issue that would bring great comfort to his wife and daughter after his death. Knowing he would not live long enough to see his plan fulfilled, he wrote a letter for his successor:

> "I entirely acquiesce in the betrothal of your second sister with Prince Alexander of Battenberg. I charge you as a filial duty with the accomplishment of this

my desire, which your sister Victoria [Moretta] for so many years has cherished in her heart."[319]

On 1st June, he withdrew from Berlin to his favourite home, the New Palace in Potsdam, which, on his accession, he had renamed *Schloss Friedrichskron*. For ease and comfort, he travelled by boat and, as he emerged from his cabin, a witness on the pier observed that he was 'crouched down, wretched, scared, and pallid, like a man going to execution.'[320]

A few days later, Vicky reported to her mother that Fritz 'is doing rather well today' but it was only a brief respite in a week of rapid decline. On 8th June, while he was eating porridge, milk trickled out of his canula, giving rise to the fear that food would enter his windpipe. When all other efforts to resolve the problem had failed, the doctors decided to feed him by means of a tube, which caused him even greater discomfort and further hindered his breathing.

On 12th June, he briefly received King Oscar of Sweden, but in the early hours of the following morning, his breathing became so laboured that Mackenzie woke Vicky to warn her that the end was imminent. On 14th June, he sent for his daughter, Sophie, so that he could present her with the flowers that he had ordered for her birthday; and, from then onwards, Vicky never left his side, holding his hand as he lingered, fully conscious, for a further twenty-four hours.

A grey and rainy morning dawned on 15th June and, shortly after eleven o'clock, the laboured breathing ceased, Fritz eyes glazed over, and his long and arduous ordeal was complete.

> "Thus passed away," wrote Mackenzie, "the noblest specimen of humanity it has ever been my privilege to know."[321]

His body was wrapped in his military cloak, and Vicky personally placed his sword in his hand; and, on his breast she laid his insignia *Pour la Merité,* and a victory wreath that she had made for him on his return from the Franco-Prussian War.

Epilogue

Fritz' funeral took place on 18th June in the Friedenskirche in Potsdam, where his sons, Sigismund and Waldemar, had been interred. After days of rain, the sun shone brightly on the rows and rows of cuirassiers, guards, infantrymen and cavalrymen, who marched in a slow procession, headed by Fritz' faithful warhorse – Worth, named after the victorious battle.

On the same day, Lord Salisbury gave a moving address to the House of Lords:

"He has left an example which may be of most precious value, not only to sovereigns and those who may follow him, but to all sorts and conditions of men; and it is with a feeling that we are performing no act of mere formality in rendering homage to one of the highest and noblest natures which ever adorned a throne, that I move the addresses which I have now the honour of laying on the table."[322]

Queen Victoria, privately weeping alone, thought back through the years and sighed, 'He was so kind to me always...I see him always before me with those beautiful loving blue eyes."[323]

Even his fiercest critics confessed that he had nobly borne his illness with stoicism, courage and fortitude; and, despite Bismarck's attempts to claim all the glory, they could not underestimate Fritz' role in bringing about German unification. Nonetheless, as the eulogies faded, some asked what he had achieved in the seventeen years since the Franco-Prussian War.

"It is fair to reflect," an American journalist wrote in 1891, "...that this fine, handsome, able, and good-hearted Prince could not have created for himself such hosts of hostile critics in his own country, could not have continually found himself year by year losing his hold upon even the minority of his fellow-countrymen, without reason. It is certain that in 1886 – the year before his illness befell – he had come to a minimum of usefulness, influence, and popularity in the Empire."[324]

Perhaps his critics failed to take into account his 'unsanguine temperament' and his proneness to depression. When he failed to receive recognition for his greatest achievement – his role in unification – he appeared to have given up hope of contributing to affairs of state during his father's reign, and to resign himself to biding his time until his own accession. No one would have suspected that Emperor William I would have lived for so long, since, as early as 1870, he had major health concerns, but, as the years went by, Fritz sank more frequently into depression, exacerbated by inaction and tensions within his own home.

More pertinently, throughout so much of his life, he found himself between opposing factions, and his only means of maintaining peace was to remain silent. As a child, unwilling to offend his liberal mother or to contradict his militaristic father, he had made a point of not expressing any controversial opinion; and, as a young man in a patriotic court, he had been unable to voice his growing love for England. Following his father's accession, loyalty and filial duty prevented him from speaking out against the Emperor's policies; and, on the one occasion when he dared to do so[ww], he was racked with guilt and 'almost broken-hearted at causing his father so much pain'[325]. Only on the battlefield could he speak with the voice of authority but, when the war was over, he withdrew into his customary taciturnity, and the speeches that he was required to make were delivered in an uninspiring monotone. The tragic irony was that, when he was finally

---

[ww] See Chapter 8

in a position to speak with authority, cancer had left him barely able to utter a word.

Vicky's long-running dispute with William continued for several years after his accession, but, although they never enjoyed a close relationship, they eventually settled into mutual acceptance. She retired from Berlin to Krönberg in the Taunus Mountains, where she renovated a dilapidated property, which she named Friedrichshof in Fritz' memory. In his honour, too, she contributed to a new hospital in San Remo, designed for patients with contagious diseases and those who could not afford any other treatment. She continued her many philanthropic activities and devoted much of her time to her family. In 1899, she was diagnosed with breast cancer which had spread to her spine; and she died in August 1901 – seven months after the death of Queen Victoria.

In 1903, William unveiled a bronze statue of his mother in her coronation robes opposite a similar monument to his father. In his memoirs he wrote that she had been:

"…a woman of great gifts, full of ideas and initiative. If, however, she was never quite appreciated as she deserved…I am convinced that history will give her the full recognition that, like so much else, was dirtied in her lifetime."[326]

In spite of Fritz' final request, William did not give his sister permission to marry Sandro Battenberg, who, as Queen Victoria knew, had already abandoned all thoughts of Moretta, having fallen in love with actress whom he subsequently married. Only four years later, in 1893, he died at the age of only thirty-six.

Moretta eventually married a 'rather scruffy' and impoverished prince, Adolph of Schaumburg-Lippe, and, although it was widely believed that she had accepted his proposal out of desperation, observers were surprised to see that the couple appeared happy together:

> "They seem a very devoted couple," wrote a lady-in-waiting when they visited Windsor in 1898, "and she has changed much and for the better in her personal appearance, being now a graceful, good-looking woman instead of a particularly plain girl."[327]

On his accession, William retained Bismarck's services as Chancellor but he was soon exasperated by the statesman's constant undermining of his orders and his underhand methods. Matters came to a head in 1890 when, following a violent argument, William insisted that he should offer his resignation. Remarkably, Bismarck turned to Vicky for help, asking her to persuade her son to reinstate him. Perhaps she gained some satisfaction in explaining that, thanks to Bismarck's constant meddling in her family affairs, she longer had any influence over William. Bismarck retired to the country estate where he wrote his memoirs, presenting himself in a favourable light throughout all his years of service. He died in 1898, at the age of eighty-three.

By The Same Author:

Biography & History
Queen Victoria's Granddaughters 1960-1918
Queen Victoria's Grandsons 1859-1918
Queen Victoria's Cousins
Queen Victoria's Creatures – Royalty & Animals in the Victoria Era
Alice, the Enigma – A Biography of Queen Victoria's Daughter
Dear Papa, Beloved Mama – An intimate portrait of Queen Victoria & Prince Albert as parents
The Innocence of Kaiser Wilhelm II
Queen Victoria & The French Royal Families
Thunder of Freedom – The British Suffragette Movement
Queen Victoria & Her Prime Ministers

Historical Fiction
Most Beautiful Princess – A Novel Based on the Life of Grand Duchess Elizabeth of Russia
Shattered Crowns: The Scapegoats
Shattered Crowns: The Sacrifice
Shattered Crowns: The Betrayal
The Fields Laid Waste

Novels
The Counting House
By Any Other Name
The Goose Girl

Poetry & Children's Books
Wonderful Walter
Child of the Moon
The Ragamuffin Sun

[1] Fulford, Roger (editor) *Beloved Mama: Private Correspondence of Queen Victoria and the German Crown Princess 1878-1885* (Evans Bros 1981)
[2] Tschudi, Clara (translated by E.M. Cope) *Augusta, Empress of Germany* (E. Dutton 1900)
[3] Radziwill, Princess Catherine *My Recollections* (Sir Isaac Pitman & Sons 1906)
[4] Eylert, Bishop, translated by Jonathan Birch *Frederick William III, King of Prussia* (George Bell 1845)
[5] Barkeley, Richard *Empress Frederick* (Macmillan & Co. 1956)
[6] Radziwill, Princess Catherine *Those I Remember* (Small, Maynard & Co. 1914)
[7] Gower, Ronald Sutherland *My Reminiscences* (Kegan, Paul & Trenchard 1883)
[8] Rennell Rodd, James *Frederick, Crown Prince & Emperor* (Macmillan 1888)
[9] Fulford, Roger (editor) *Dearest Child: Letters Between Queen Victoria & the Princess Royal 1858-1861* (Evans 1964)
[10] Fulford, Roger (editor) *Dearest Child: Letters Between Queen Victoria & the Princess Royal 1858-1861* (Evans 1964)
[11] Fulford, Roger (editor) *Beloved Mama: Private Correspondence of Queen Victoria and the German Crown Princess 1878-1885* (Evans Bros 1981)
[12] Poschinger, Margarethe von *Life of Emperor Frederick* (Harper & Bros. 1901)
[13] Bennett, Daphne *King Without a Crown* (William Heinemann 1977)
[14] Radziwill, Princess Catherine *Memories of Forty Years* (Funk & Wagnalls 1915)
[15] Topham, Anne *Memories of the Kaiser's Court* (Dodd, Mead & Co. 1914)
[16] Martineau, Harriet *Biographical Sketches* (Macmillan 1885)
[17] Radziwill, Catherine *Sovereigns & Statesmen of Europe* (Funk & Wangalls 1916)
[18] Perris, George Herbert *Germany and the German Emperor* (Andrew Melrose Ltd. 1914)
[19] Lyttelton, Sarah (edited by Mrs H. Wyndham) *Correspondence of Sarah Spencer, Lady Lyttelton* (John Murray 1912)
[20] Bunsen, Frances *A Memoir of Baron Bunsen Vol 1* (Longmans, Green & Co. 1868)
[21] Martineau, Harriet *Biographical Sketches* (Macmillan 1885)
[22] Loftus, Augustus *The Diplomatic Reminiscences of Lord Augustus Loftus Vol. 1* (Cassell & Co. 1892)
[23] Bolitho, Hector *Further Letters of Queen Victoria* (Thornton Butterworth 1938)
[24] Hare, Augustus J.C. *The Life and Letters of Frances Baroness Bunsen* (Smith, Elder & Co. 1882)
[25] Stockmar, Ernest von *Memoirs of Baron Stockmar Vol II* (Longmans, Green & Co. 1873)
[26] Lane-Poole, Stanley *The Life of the Right Honourable Stratford Canning Vol. 2* (Longmans, Green & Co. 1888)
[27] Hare, Augustus J.C. *The Life and Letters of Frances Baroness Bunsen* (Smith, Elder & Co. 1882)
[28] Chase, William S. *1848, A Year of Revolutions* (Henry E. Robins & Co. 1850)
[29] Esher, Viscount (editor) *The Letters of Queen Victoria Vol 2* (Longmans, Green & Co. 1907)
[30] Poschinger, Margarethe von *Life of Emperor Frederick* (Harper & Bros. 1901)
[31] Bismarck, Otto von *Bismarck, the Man and the Statesman Vol 1* (Smith, Elder & Co. 1898)
[32] Sylva Carmen (Queen Elisabeth of Roumania) *From Memory's Shrine* (J.P. Lippincott Company 1911)
[33] Rennell Rodd, James *Frederick, Crown Prince & Emperor* (Macmillan 1888)
[34] Bennett, Daphne *King Without A Crown* (William Heinemann 1977)
[35] Jagow, Kurt (editor), Dugdale, E. (translator) *Letters of the Prince Consort* (John Murray 1938)
[36] Jagow, Kurt (editor), Dugdale, E. (translator) *Letters of the Prince Consort* (John

Murray 1938)
[37] Lyttelton, Baroness *Letters from Sarah, Lady Lyttelton 1797-1870* (Spottiswoode & Co. 1873)
[38] Keeling, Anne E. *Great Britain & Her Queen* (1897)
[39] Bolitho, Hector *Further Letters of Queen Victoria* (Thornton Butterworth 1938)
[40] Jagow, Kurt (editor), Dugdale, E. (translator) *Letters of the Prince Consort* (John Murray 1938)
[41] Jagow, Kurt (editor), Dugdale, E. (translator) *Letters of the Prince Consort* (John Murray 1938)
[42] Benson, Arthur & Esher, Viscount *The Letters of Queen Victoria Vol III* (John Murray 1908)
[43] Sheppard, Edgar *George, Duke of Cambridge* (Longmans, Green & Co. 1906)
[44] Maxwell, Sir Herbert *The Life and Letters of George William Frederick, Fourth Earl of Clarendon, K.G., G.C.B.* (Edward Arnold 1913)
[45] Keeling, Anne E. *Great Britain & Her Queen* (1897)
[46] Barkeley, Richard *The Empress Frederick* (MacMillan & Co. 1956)
[47] Maxwell, Sir Herbert *The Life and Letters of George William Frederick, Fourth Earl of Clarendon, K.G., G.C.B.* (Edward Arnold 1913)
[48] Benson, Arthur C. *The Letters of Queen Victoria, Vol. II A Selection from Her Majesty's Correspondence Between the Years 1837 and 1861*
[49] Maxwell, Sir Herbert *The Life and Letters of George William Frederick, Fourth Earl of Clarendon, K.G., G.C.B.* (Edward Arnold 1913)
[50] Esher, Viscount (editor) *The Letters of Queen Victoria Vol 3* (Longmans, Green & Co. 1907)
[51] Anonymous *Empress Frederick, A Memoir* (Dodd, Mead and Co. 1914)
[52] Ponsonby, Frederick (editor) *Letters of the Empress Frederick* (Macmillan & Co. 1928)
[53] Stanley, The Hon. Eleanor (Edited by Mrs Stuart Erskine) *Twenty Years at Court* (Nisbet & Co. 1918)
[54] Stanley, The Hon. Eleanor (Edited by Mrs Stuart Erskine) *Twenty Years at Court* (Nisbet & Co. 1918)
[55] Paget, Walburga *Scenes & Memories* (Charles Scribner's Sons 1912)
[56] Ponsonby, Arthur *Henry Ponsonby, Queen Victoria's Private Secretary* (Macmillan & Co. 1942)
[57] Jagow, Kurt (editor), Dugdale, E. (translator) *Letters of the Prince Consort* (John Murray 1938)
[58] Bolitho, Hector *Further Letters of Queen Victoria* (Thornton Butterworth 1938)
[59] https://henrypoole.com/individual/grand-duke-frederick-i-of-baden
[60] Paget, Walburga *Scenes & Memories* (Charles Scribner's Sons 1912)
[61] Kinlock Cooke, C. *A Memoir of Her Royal Highness, Princess Mary Adelaide Vol 1* (John Murray 1901)
[62] Sheppard, Edgar *George, Duke of Cambridge* (Longmans, Green & Co. 1906)
[63] Greville, Charles *A Journal of the Reign of Queen Victoria Vol 1* (Longmans, Green & Co, 1887)
[64] Boyd Carpenter, William *Some Pages of My Life* (Williams & Norgate 1911)
[65] Kinlock Cooke, C. *A Memoir of Her Royal Highness, Princess Mary Adelaide Vol 1* (John Murray 1901)
[66] Anonymous *Empress Frederick, A Memoir* (Dodd, Mead and Co. 1914)
[67] Paget, Walburga *Scenes & Memories* (Charles Scribner's Sons 1912)
[68] Fane, Lady Rose (editor) *The Correspondence of Priscilla, Countess of Westmorland* (E.F. Dutton 1909)
[69] Fulford, Roger (editor) *Dearest Child: Letters Between Queen Victoria & the Princess Royal 1858-1861* (Evans 1964)

[70] Paget, Walburga *Scenes & Memories* (Charles Scribner's Sons 1912)
[71] Hamilton, Lord Frederic *The Vanished Pomps of Yesterday* (G.H. Doran 1921)
[72] Marie Louise, Princess *My Memories of Six Reigns* (Evans Brothers 1956)
[73] Benson, E.F. *The Kaiser & English Relations* (Longmans, Green & Co. 1936)
[74] Jersey, Dowager Countess of *Fifty-One Years of Victorian Life* (E.P. Dutton & Company 1922)
[75] Fulford, Roger (editor) *Your Dear Letter; Private Correspondence of Queen Victoria and the Crown Princess of Prussia 1865-1871* (Evans 1971)
[76] Fulford, Roger (Editor) *Dearest Child, Letters between Queen Victoria & the Princess Royal 1858-1861* (Evans Brothers 1964)
[77] Fulford, Roger (Editor) *Dearest Child, Letters between Queen Victoria & the Princess Royal 1858-1861* (Evans Brothers 1964)
[78] Paget, Walburga *Scenes & Memories* (Charles Scribner's Sons 1912)
[79] Poschinger, Margarethe von *Life of Emperor Frederick* (Harper & Bros. 1901)
[80] Fulford, Roger (editor) *Dearest Child: Letters Between Queen Victoria & the Princess Royal 1858-1861* (Evans 1964)
[81] Fane, Lady Rose (editor) *The Correspondence of Priscilla, Countess of Westmorland* (E.F. Dutton 1909)
[82] Lowe, Charles *The German Emperor, William II* (Bliss, Sands & Foster 1895)
[83] Paget, Walburga *Scenes & Memories* (Charles Scribner's Sons 1912)
[84] Jersey, Dowager Countess of *Fifty-One Years of Victorian Life* (E.P. Dutton & Company 1922)
[85] Hamilton, Lord Frederic *The Vanished Pomps of Yesterday* (G.H. Doran 1921)
[86] Forbes, Archibald *William of Germany* (Cassell & Co. 1888)
[87] Wemys, Rosalind *Memoirs and Letters of the Right Hon. Sir Robert Morier, G.C.B., from 1826 to 1876* (Edward Arnold 1911)
[88] Fulford, Roger (editor) *Dearest Child: Letters Between Queen Victoria & the Princess Royal 1858-1861* (Evans 1964)
[89] Jagow, Kurt (editor), Dugdale, E. (translator) *Letters of the Prince Consort* (John Murray 1938)
[90] Fulford, Roger (editor) *Dearest Child: Letters Between Queen Victoria & the Princess Royal 1858-1861* (Evans 1964)
[91] Radziwill, Catherine *Sovereigns & Statesmen of Europe* (Funk & Wangalls 1916)
[92] Anonymous *Empress Frederick, A Memoir* (Dodd, Mead and Co. 1914)
[93] Jagow, Kurt (editor), Dugdale, E. (translator) *Letters of the Prince Consort* (John Murray 1938)
[94] Abeken, Heinrich, Barrett-Lennnard, Mrs Charles (translator) *Bismarck's Pen, The Life of Heinrich Abeken* (George Allen & Co. 1911)
[95] Abeken, Heinrich, Barrett-Lennnard, Mrs Charles (translator) *Bismarck's Pen, The Life of Heinrich Abeken* (George Allen & Co. 1911)
[96] Maxwell, Sir Herbert *The Life and Letters of George William Frederick, Fourth Earl of Clarendon, K.G., G.C.B.* (Edward Arnold 1913)
[97] Paget, Walburga *Scenes & Memories* (Charles Scribner's Sons 1912)
[98] Bismarck, Otto von (translated by A.J. Butler) *Bismarck, the Man & the Statesman* (Harper & Brothers 1898)
[99] Wycliffe Headlam, James *Bismarck & The Foundation of the German Empire* (G.P. Putnam's Sons 1911)
[100] Ford, J.A. (translator) *The Correspondence of William I & Bismarck* (F.A. Stokes Co. 1903)
[101] Radziwill, Catherine *Sovereigns & Statesmen of Europe* (Funk & Wangalls 1916)
[102] Wycliffe Headlam, James *Bismarck & The Foundation of the German Empire* (G.P. Putnam's Sons 1911)
[103] Poschinger, Margarethe von *Life of Emperor Frederick* (Harper & Bros. 1901)

[104] Poschinger, Margarethe von *Life of Emperor Frederick* (Harper & Bros. 1901)
[105] Ford, J.A. (translator) *The Correspondence of William I & Bismarck* (F.A. Stokes Co. 1903)
[106] Ponsonby, Frederick (editor) *Letters of the Empress Frederick* (Macmillan & Co. 1928)
[107] Steefel, Lawrence D. *The Schleswig-Holstein Question* (Cambridge University Press 1932)
[108] Ponsonby, Frederick (editor) *The Letters of the Empress Frederick* (Macmillan & Co. 1928)
[109] Lang, Andrew (editor) *Life, Letters, and Diaries of Sir Stafford Northcote, 1st Earl of Iddesleigh* (William Blackwood & Sons 1891)
[110] Maxwell, Sir Herbert *The Life and Letters of George William Frederick, Fourth Earl of Clarendon, K.G., G.C.B.* (Edward Arnold 1913)
[111] Ford, J.A. (translator) *The Correspondence of William I & Bismarck* (F.A. Stokes Co. 1903)
[112] Steefel, Lawrence D. *The Schleswig-Holstein Question* (Cambridge University Press 1932)
[113] Steefel, Lawrence D. *The Schleswig-Holstein Question* (Cambridge University Press 1932)
[114] Wemys, Rosslyn, *The Memoirs and Letters of Sir Robert Morier Vol 2* (Edward Arnold 1911)
[115] Lee, Sir Sidney *King Edward VII Vol 2* (Macmillan & Co. 1925)
[116] Fontenoy, Marquise de *Revelation of High Life Within Royal Palaces* (Edgewood Publishing Company 1892)
[117] Poschinger, Margarethe von *Life of Emperor Frederick* (Harper & Bros. 1901)
[118] Christian, Princess (editor) *Alice, Grand Duchess of Hesse, Princess of Great Britain and Ireland* (John Murray 1884)
[119] Ponsonby, Frederick (editor) *The Letters of the Empress Frederick* (Macmillan & Co. 1928)
[120] Maxwell, Sir Herbert *The Life and Letters of George William Frederick, Fourth Earl of Clarendon, K.G., G.C.B.* (Edward Arnold 1913)
[121] Buckle, George Earle (editor) *The Letters of Queen Victoria 1862-1869 Vol 1* (John Murray 1926)
[122] Maxwell, Sir Herbert *The Life and Letters of George William Frederick, Fourth Earl of Clarendon, K.G., G.C.B.* (Edward Arnold 1913)
[123] Rennell Rodd, James *Frederick, Crown Prince & Emperor* (Macmillan 1888)
[124] Hozier, H.M. *The Franco-Prussian War* (W. Mackenzie 1872)
[125] Beauchamp Walker, C.P. *Days of a Soldier's Life* (Chapman & Hall 1894)
[126] Blumenthal, Count von; Gillespie Addison, A.D. (translator) *Journals of Field-Marshall Count von Blumenthal for 1866 and 1870-71* (Edward Arnold 1903)
[127] Hozier, H.M. *The Seven Weeks' War & Its Incidents* (Macmillan & Co. 1871)
[128] Sheppard, Edgar *George, Duke of Cambridge* (Longmans, Green & Co. 1906)
[129] Blumenthal, Count von; Gillespie Addison, A.D. (translator) *Journals of Field-Marshall Count von Blumenthal for 1866 and 1870-71* (Edward Arnold 1903)
[130] Whitman, Sydney *Personal Reminiscences of Prince Bismarck* (John Murray 1902)
[131] Bismarck, Otto von (translated by A.J. Butler) *Bismarck, the Man & the Statesman* (Harper & Brothers 1898)
[132] Rennell Rodd, James *Frederick, Crown Prince & Emperor* (Macmillan 1888)
[133] Poschinger, Margarethe von *Life of Emperor Frederick* (Harper & Bros. 1901)
[134] Ponsonby, Frederick (editor) *The Letters of the Empress Frederick* (Macmillan & Co. 1928)
[135] Abeken, Heinrich, Barrett-Lennnard, Mrs Charles (translator) *Bismarck's Pen, The Life of Heinrich Abeken* (George Allen & Co. 1911)

[136] Bolitho, Hector *The Reign of Queen Victoria* (Macmillan 1948)
[137] Bismarck, Otto von *Bismarck, the Man and the Statesman Vol 1* (Smith, Elder & Co. 1898)
[138] Perris, George Herbert *Germany and the German Emperor* (Andrew Melrose Ltd. 1914)
[139] Fulford, Roger (editor) *Your Dear Letter; Private Correspondence of Queen Victoria and the Crown Princess of Prussia 1865-1871* (Evans 1971)
[140] Wemys, Rosslyn, *The Memoirs and Letters of Sir Robert Morier Vol 2* (Edward Arnold 1911)
[141] Rennell Rodd, James *Frederick, Crown Prince & Emperor* (Macmillan 1888)
[142] Wilson, Arnold T. *The Suez Canal* (Oxford University Press 1930)
[143] Beauchamp Walker, C.P. *Days of a Soldier's Life* (Chapman & Hall 1894)
[144] Radziwill, Catherine *Those I Remember* (Small, Maynard & Co. 1914)
[145] Fulford, Roger (editor) *Your Dear Letter; Private Correspondence of Queen Victoria and the Crown Princess of Prussia 1865-1871* (Evans 1971)
[146] Fulford, Roger (editor) *Your Dear Letter; Private Correspondence of Queen Victoria and the Crown Princess of Prussia 1865-1871* (Evans 1971)
[147] Fulford, Roger (editor) *Your Dear Letter; Private Correspondence of Queen Victoria and the Crown Princess of Prussia 1865-1871* (Evans 1971)
[148] Fulford, Roger (editor) *Your Dear Letter; Private Correspondence of Queen Victoria and the Crown Princess of Prussia 1865-1871* (Evans 1971)
[149] Fulford, Roger (editor) *Your Dear Letter; Private Correspondence of Queen Victoria and the Crown Princess of Prussia 1865-1871* (Evans 1971)
[150] Fulford, Roger (editor) *Your Dear Letter; Private Correspondence of Queen Victoria and the Crown Princess of Prussia 1865-1871* (Evans 1971)
[151] Lowe, Charles *The German Emperor, William II* (Bliss, Sands & Foster 1895)
[152] Radziwill, Catherine *Those I Remember* (Small, Maynard & Co. 1914)
[153] Ponsonby, Frederick (editor) *Letters of the Empress Frederick* (Macmillan & Co. 1928)
[154] Helena Victoria, Princess (editor) *Alice Grand Duchess of Hesse, Biographical Sketch and Letters* (John Murray 1884)
[155] Pope-Hennessy, Jame (editor) *Queen Victoria at Balmoral & Windsor* (George Allen & Unwin 1959)
[156] Fulford, Roger (editor) *Beloved Mama: Private Correspondence of Queen Victoria and the German Crown Princess 1878-1885* (Evans Bros 1981)
[157] Fulford, Roger (editor) *Beloved Mama: Private Correspondence of Queen Victoria and the German Crown Princess 1878-1885* (Evans Bros 1981)
[158] Anon *The Empress Frederick: A Memoir* (James Nisbet & Co. 1913)
[159] Rodd, Rennell *Frederick Crown Prince & Emperor ; A Biographical Sketch Dedicated to His Memory* (D. Stott 1888)
[160] Bigelow, Poultney *The German Emperor* (New Review, August 1889)
[161] Schwering, Count Axel von *The Berlin Court Under William II* (Cassell & Company Limited 1915)
[162] Wilhelm II, *My Early Life* (G.H. Doran 1926)
[163] Walpole, Sir Spencer *History of Twenty-Five Years Vol. 2* (Longmans, Green & Co. 1904)
[164] Trollope, Anthony *Lord Palmerston* (W. Isbister, 1882)
[165] Poschinger, Margarete (translated by Sidney Whitman) *Life of the Emperor Frederick* (Harper & Bros. 1901)
[166] Paléologue, Maurice *The Tragic Empress; Intimate Conversations with the Empress Eugénie, 1901-1911* (Thornton Butterworth 1920)
[167] Fulford, Roger (editor) *Your Dear Letter; Private Correspondence of Queen Victoria and the Crown Princess of Prussia 1865-1871* (Evans 1971)

[168] Evans, Thomas Wiltberger (edited by Edward Crane) *Memoirs of Dr Thomas Evans: The Second Empire* (D. Appleton & Co. 1905)
[169] Fleury, Comte Maurice *Memoirs of the Empress Eugénie* (D. Appleton & Co. 1920)
[170] Benedetti, Count Vincent *Studies in Diplomacy* (Macmillan 1896)
[171] Helena Victoria, Princess (editor) *Alice Grand Duchess of Hesse, Biographical Sketch and Letters* (John Murray 1884)
[172] Fontenoy, Marquise de *Revelation of High Life Within Royal Palaces* (Edgewood Publishing Company 1892)
[173] Ponsonby, Frederick (editor) *The Letters of the Empress Frederick* (Macmillan & Co. 1928)
[174] Russell, Sir William Howard *My Diary during the Last Great War* (G. Routledge & Sons 1874)
[175] Frederick III *The Suppressed Diary of the late Emperor Frederick* (1888)
[176] Hozier, H.M. *The Franco-Prussian War* (W. Mackenzie 1872)
[177] Ollier, Edmund *History of the War Between France & Germany Vol 1*, (Cassell & co. 1874)
[178] Fontenoy, Marquise de *Revelation of High Life Within Royal Palaces* (Edgewood Publishing Company 1892)
[179] Blumenthal, Count von; Gillespie Addison, A.D. (translator) *Journals of Field-Marshall Count von Blumenthal for 1866 and 1870-71* (Edward Arnold 1903)
[180] Russell, Sir William Howard *My Diary during the Last Great War* (G. Routledge & Sons 1874)
[181] Frederick III *The Suppressed Diary of the late Emperor Frederick* (1888)
[182] Blumenthal, Count von; Gillespie Addison, A.D. (translator) *Journals of Field-Marshall Count von Blumenthal for 1866 and 1870-71* (Edward Arnold 1903)
[183] Helps, Arthur *The Correspondence of Sir Arthur Helps* (Bodley Head 1917)
[184] Fulford, Roger (editor) *Your Dear Letter; Private Correspondence of Queen Victoria and the Crown Princess of Prussia 1865-1871* (Evans 1971)
[185] Russell, Sir William Howard *My Diary during the Last Great War* (G. Routledge & Sons 1874)
[186] Sheppard, Edgar *George, Duke of Cambridge* (Longmans, Green & Co. 1906)
[187] Lano, Pierre de (translated by Ethelred Taylor) *Empress Eugenie* (Dodd, Mead & Co. 1894)
[188] Fleury, Comte *Memoirs of the Empress Eugenie Vol II* (D. Appleton & Co.)
[189] Frederick III, German Emperor *The Suppressed Diary of Frederick III* (Pall Mall Gazette 1888)
[190] Fleury, Comte *Memoirs of the Empress Eugenie Vol II* (D. Appleton & Co.)
[191] Rennell Rodd, James *Frederick, Crown Prince & Emperor* (Macmillan 1888)
[192] Ollier, Edmund *History of the War Between France & Germany Vol 1*, (Cassell & co. 1874)
[193] Cerf, Barry *Alsace-Lorraine Since 1870* (The Macmillan Company 1919)
[194] Russell, Sir William Howard *My Diary during the Last Great War* (G. Routledge & Sons 1874)
[195] Barkeley, Richard *The Empress Frederick* (Macmillan 1956)
[196] Rennell Rodd, James *Frederick, Crown Prince & Emperor* (Macmillan 1888)
[197] Holland, Caroline *The Notebooks of a Spinster Lady* (Cassell & Co. 1919)
[198] Buckle, George (editor) *The Letters of Queen Victoria Vol. 2* (John Murray 1926)
[199] Buckle, George (editor) *The Letters of Queen Victoria Vol. 2* (John Murray 1926)
[200] Labouchere, Henri du Pré *Diary of the Besieged Resident in Paris* (Hurst & Blackett 1871)
[201] Wycliffe Headlam, James *Bismarck & The Foundation of the German Empire* (G.P. Putnam's Sons 1911)
[202] Frederick III, Emperor; Welby, Frances (translator) *Diaries of the Emperor Frederick*

(Chapman & Hall 1902)
[203] Frederick III, Emperor; Welby, Frances (translator) *Diaries of the Emperor Frederick* (Chapman & Hall 1902)
[204] Hohenlohe-Schillingsfurst, Chlodwig of *Memoirs of Prince Chlodwig of Hohenlohe-Schillingsfurst* (William Heinemann 1906)
[205] Tschudi, Clara; Hearn, Ethel Harriet (translator) *Ludwig the Second, King of Bavaria* (S. Sonnenschein & Co. Ltd. 1908)
[206] Frederick III, Emperor; Welby, Frances (translator) *Diaries of the Emperor Frederick* (Chapman & Hall 1902)
[207] Buckle, George (editor) *The Letters of Queen Victoria Vol. 2* (John Murray 1926)
[208] Frederick III, Emperor; Welby, Frances (translator) *Diaries of the Emperor Frederick* (Chapman & Hall 1902)
[209] Radziwill, Catherine *Germany Under Three Emperors* (Funk and Wangals 1917)
[210] Radziwill, Catherine *Those I Remember* (Small Maynard 1914)
[211] Rennell Rodd, James *Social And Diplomatic Memories 1884-1893* (Edward Arnold & Co. 1922)
[212] Radziwill, Catherine *Sovereigns & Statesmen of Europe* (Funk & Wangalls 1916)
[213] Frederic, Harold *The Young Emperor, William II* (G.P. Putnam's Sons 1891)
[214] Taffs, Winnifred *Ambassador to Bismarck* (Frederick Muller Ltd. 1938)
[215] Ponsonby, Frederick (editor) *The Letters of the Empress Frederick* (Macmillan & Co. 1928)
[216] Beauchamp Walker, C.P. *Days of a Soldier's Life* (Chapman & Hall 1894)
[217] Rich, Norman & Fisher, M.H. (editors) *The Holstein Papers Vol II* (Cambridge University Press 1957)
[218] Ludwig, Emil *Kaiser Wilhelm II* (translated by Ethel Colburn Mayne) (G.P. Putnam's Sons Ltd. 1926)
[219] Hamilton, Lord Frederic *The Vanished Pomps of Yesterday* (G.H. Doran 1921)
[220] Rich, Norman & Fisher, M.H. (editors) *The Holstein Papers Vol II* (Cambridge University Press 1957)
[221] Rich, Norman & Fisher, M.H. (editors) *The Holstein Papers Vol II* (Cambridge University Press 1957)
[222] Beauchamp Walker, C.P. *Days of a Soldier's Life* (Chapman & Hall 1894)
[223] Bismarck, Otto von (translated by A.J. Butler) *Bismarck, the Man & the Statesman* (Harper & Brothers 1898)
[224] Hohenlohe-Schillingsfurst, Chlodwig of *Memoirs of Prince Chlodwig of Hohenlohe-Schillingsfurst* (William Heinemann 1906)
[225] Roumania, Marie, Queen of *The Story of My Life* (Charles Scribner's Sons 1934)
[226] Barkeley, Richard *Empress Frederick* (Macmillan & Co. 1956)
[227] Simon, Édouard *Emperor William & His Reign Vol 2* (Remington & Co. 1886)
[228] Bismarck, Otto von (translated by A.J. Butler) *Bismarck, the Man & the Statesman* (Harper & Brothers 1898)
[229] Fulford, Roger (editor) *Beloved Mama: Private Correspondence of Queen Victoria and the German Crown Princess 1878-1885* (Evans Bros 1981)
[230] Fulford, Roger (editor) *Beloved Mama: Private Correspondence of Queen Victoria and the German Crown Princess 1878-1885* (Evans Bros 1981)
[231] Ponsonby, Frederick (editor) *The Letters of the Empress Frederick* (Macmillan & Co. 1928)
[232] Fulford, Roger (editor) *Beloved Mama: Private Correspondence of Queen Victoria and the German Crown Princess 1878-1885* (Evans Bros 1981)
[233] Wilhelm II, Kaiser *My Early Life* (George H. Doran & Company 1926)
[234] *The Times* (4th April 1879)
[235] Tschudi, Clara (translated by E.M. Cope) *Augusta, Empress of Germany* (E. Dutton 1900)

[236] Hohenlohe-Schillingsfurst, Chlodwig of *Memoirs of Prince Chlodwig of Hohenlohe-Schillingsfurst* (William Heinemann 1906)
[237] Rich, Norman & Fisher, M.H. (editors) *The Holstein Papers Vol II* (Cambridge University Press 1957)
[238] Rich, Norman & Fisher, M.H. (editors) *The Holstein Papers Vol II* (Cambridge University Press 1957)
[239] Fulford, Roger (editor) *Beloved Mama: Private Correspondence of Queen Victoria and the German Crown Princess 1878-1885* (Evans Bros 1981)
[240] Rennell Rodd, James *Frederick, Crown Prince & Emperor* (Macmillan 1888)
[241] Rich, Norman & Fisher, M.H. (editors) *The Holstein Papers Vol II* (Cambridge University Press 1957)
[242] Simpson, William *The Autobiography of William Simpson* (T. Fisher, Unwin 1903)
[243] *The Times, Berlin* (1st February 1883)
[244] Fulford, Roger (editor) *Beloved Mama: Private Correspondence of Queen Victoria and the German Crown Princess 1878-1885* (Evans Bros 1981)
[245] Rennell Rodd, James *Social And Diplomatic Memories 1884-1893* (Edward Arnold & Co. 1922)
[246] Ponsonby, Arthur *Henry Ponsonby, Queen Victoria's Private Secretary* (Macmillan & Co. 1942)
[247] Radziwill, Princess Catherine *Those I Remember* (Small, Maynard & Co. 1914)
[248] Sherwood, Mrs M.E.W. *Royal Girls & Royal Courts* (D. Lothrop Company 1887)
[249] Vasili, Comte Paul *La Société de Berlin* (Nouvelle Revue 1886)
[250] Fulford, Roger (editor) *Beloved Mama: Private Correspondence of Queen Victoria and the German Crown Princess 1878-1885* (Evans Bros 1981)
[251] Ludwig, Emil (translated by Ethel Colburn Mayne) *Kaiser Wilhelm II* (G.P. Putnam's Sons Ltd. 1926)
[252] Wile, F. W. *Men Around the Kaiser* (William Heinemann 1913)
[253] Ludwig, Emil (translated by Ethel Colburn Mayne) *Kaiser Wilhelm II* (G.P. Putnam's Sons Ltd. 1926)
[254] Rich, Norman & Fisher, M.H. (editors) *The Holstein Papers Vol II* (Cambridge University Press 1957)
[255] Rich, Norman & Fisher, M.H. (editors) *The Holstein Papers Vol II* (Cambridge University Press 1957)
[256] Schwering, Count Axel von *The Berlin Court Under William II* (Cassell & Company Limited 1915)
[257] Rich, Norman & Fisher, M.H. (editors) *The Holstein Papers Vol II* (Cambridge University Press 1957)
[258] Ramm, Agatha *Darling & Beloved Child* (Sutton 1998)
[259] Rich, Norman & Fisher, M.H. (editors) *The Holstein Papers Vol II* (Cambridge University Press 1957)
[260] Wile, F. W. *Men Around the Kaiser* (William Heinemann 1913)
[261] Hohenlohe-Schillingsfurst, Chlodwig of *Memoirs of Prince Chlodwig of Hohenlohe-Schillingsfurst* (William Heinemann 1906)
[262] Rich, Norman & Fisher, M.H. (editors) *The Holstein Papers Vol II* (Cambridge University Press 1957)
[263] Busch, Moritz *Bismarck: Some Secret Pages of his History* (Macmillan 1898)
[264] Rich, Norman & Fisher, M.H. (editors) *The Holstein Papers Vol II* (Cambridge University Press 1957)
[265] Hohenlohe-Schillingsfurst, Chlodwig of *Memoirs of Prince Chlodwig of Hohenlohe-Schillingsfurst* (William Heinemann 1906)
[266] Busch, Moritz *Bismarck: Some Secret Pages of his History* (Macmillan 1898)
[267] Buckle, George Earle (editor) *Letters of Queen Victoria Vol 3* (John Murray 1928)
[268] Ludwig, Emil (translated by Ethel Colburn Mayne) *Kaiser Wilhelm II* (G.P. Putnam's

Sons Ltd. 1926)
[269] Rich, Norman & Fisher, M.H. (editors) *The Holstein Papers Vol II* (Cambridge University Press 1957)
[270] Ford, J.A. (translator) *The Correspondence of William I & Bismarck* (F.A. Stokes Co. 1903)
[271] Rennell Rodd, James *Social And Diplomatic Memories 1884-1893* (Edward Arnold & Co. 1922)
[272] Jersey, Dowager Countess of *Fifty-One Years of Victorian Life* (E.P. Dutton & Company 1922)
[273] Cunliffe-Owen, Marguerite *Imperator et Rex: William II* (Harper & Bros. 1904)
[274] Bismarck, Otto von *Bismarck, the Man and the Statesman Vol II* (Smith, Elder & Co. 1898)
[275] Frederic, Harold *The Young Emperor, William II* (G.P. Putnam's Sons 1891)
[276] Haweis, Rev. H.R. *Sir Morell Mackenzie; Physician and Operator* (W.H. Allen 1893)
[277] Hamilton, Lord Frederic *The Vanished Pomps of Yesterday* (G.H. Doran 1921)
[278] *The Case of Emperor Frederick III: Full Official Reports* (E.S. Werner 1888)
[279] *The Case of Emperor Frederick III: Full Official Reports* (E.S. Werner 1888)
[280] Haweis, Rev. H.R. *Sir Morell Mackenzie; Physician and Operator* (W.H. Allen 1893)
[281] *The Case of Emperor Frederick III – Full Official Reports* (1888)
[282] *The Case of Emperor Frederick III – Full Official Reports* (1888)
[283] Reid, Michaela, *Ask Sir James* (Eland 1996)
[284] Caitlin, Thomas *My Life's Pilgrimage* (John Murray 1911)
[285] *The Case of Emperor Frederick III - Full Official Reports* (1888)
[286] Roumania, Queen Marie of *The Story of My Life* (Charles Scribner's Sons 1934)
[287] Ramm, Agatha *Darling & Beloved Child* (Sutton 1998)
[288] *The Case of Emperor Frederick III – Full Official Reports* (1888)
[289] *The Case of Emperor Frederick III – Full Official Reports* (1888)
[290] Ponsonby, Magdalen (editor) *Mary Ponsonby: A Memoir, Some Letters & A Journal* (John Murray 1927)
[291] Ponsonby, Magdalen (editor) *Mary Ponsonby: A Memoir, Some Letters & A Journal* (John Murray 1927)
[292] Rich, Norman & Fisher, M.H. (editors) *The Holstein Papers Vol II* (Cambridge University Press 1957)
[293] Rich, Norman & Fisher, M.H. (editors) *The Holstein Papers Vol II* (Cambridge University Press 1957)
[294] Rennell Rodd, James *Social And Diplomatic Memories 1884-1893* (Edward Arnold & Co. 1922)
[295] Ponsonby, Magdalen (editor) *Mary Ponsonby: A Memoir, Some Letters & A Journal* (John Murray 1927)
[296] Ponsonby, Magdalen (editor) *Mary Ponsonby: A Memoir, Some Letters & A Journal* (John Murray 1927)
[297] Mackenzie, Morell *The Fatal Illness of Frederick the Noble* (Sampson Low, Marston, Searle & Rivington 1888)
[298] Ludwig, Emil (translated by Ethel Colburn Mayne) *Kaiser Wilhelm II* (G.P. Putnam's Sons Ltd. 1926)
[299] Barkeley, Richard *Empress Frederick* (Macmillan & Co. 1956)
[300] William II, Kaiser *My Early Life* (George H. Doran 1926)
[301] Reid, Michaela, *Ask Sir James* (Eland 1996)
[302] Ramm, Agatha *Darling & Beloved Child* (Sutton 1998)
[303] Barkeley, Richard *Empress Frederick* (Macmillan & Co. 1956)
[304] Ponsonby, Magdalen (editor) *Mary Ponsonby: A Memoir, Some Letters & A Journal* (John Murray 1927)
[305] Fontenoy, Marquise de *Revelation of High Life Within Royal Palaces* (Edgewood

Publishing Company 1892)
[306] Ponsonby, Magdalen (editor) *Mary Ponsonby: A Memoir, Some Letters & A Journal* (John Murray 1927)
[307] Ponsonby, Frederick (editor) *The Letters of the Empress Frederick* (Macmillan & Co. 1928)
[308] Ponsonby, Magdalen (editor) *Mary Ponsonby: A Memoir, Some Letters & A Journal* (John Murray 1927)
[309] Barkeley, Richard *The Empress Frederick* (MacMillan 1956)
[310] Ponsonby, Magdalen (editor) *Mary Ponsonby: A Memoir, Some Letters & A Journal* (John Murray 1927)
[311] Mackenzie, Morell *The Fatal Illness of Frederick the Noble* (Sampson Low, Marston, Searle & Rivington 1888)
[312] Ponsonby, Arthur *Henry Ponsonby, Queen Victoria's Private Secretary* (Macmillan & Co. 1942)
[313] Ponsonby, Arthur *Henry Ponsonby, Queen Victoria's Private Secretary* (Macmillan & Co. 1942)
[314] Cecil, Lady Gwendoline *Life of Robert, Marquis of Salisbury Vol 4* (Hodder & Stoughton 1921)
[315] Benson, E.F. *Queen Victoria* (Longmans, Green & Co. 1935)
[316] Anon *The Late Empress Frederick* (North American Review - September 1901)
[317] Ponsonby, Arthur *Henry Ponsonby, Queen Victoria's Private Secretary* (Macmillan & Co. 1942)
[318] Mackenzie, Morell *The Fatal Illness of Frederick the Noble* (Sampson Low, Marston, Searle & Rivington 1888)
[319] Ponsonby, Frederick (editor) *Letters of the Empress Frederick* (Macmillan & Co. 1928)
[320] Frederic, Harold *The Young Emperor, William II of Germany* (G.P. Putnam's Sons 1891)
[321] Mackenzie, Morell *The Fatal Illness of Frederick the Noble* (Sampson Low, Marston, Searle & Rivington 1888)
[322] Holstead, Murat & Munson, A.J. *The Life & Reign of Queen Victoria* (International Publishing Society 1901)
[323] Ramm, Agatha *Darling & Beloved Child* (Sutton 1998)
[324] Frederic, Harold *The Young Emperor, William II of Germany* (G.P. Putnam's Sons 1891)
[325] Ponsonby, Frederick (editor) *Letters of the Empress Frederick* (Macmillan & Co. 1928)
[326] Wilhelm II, *My Early Life* (G.H. Doran 1926)
[327] Mallet, Victor *Life With Queen Victoria – Marie Mallet's letters from court 1887-1901* (John Murray 1968)

Printed in Great Britain
by Amazon